Let's Play Chess!

Learn about the King, Queen, Knight, Bishop, Rook, and the many Pawns. Find out about the rules, the moves, and the strategies of this world-famous game. The author, a U.S. National Chess Master, presents a simple, numbered format that is sure to make you a winning chess player in no time at all. Chess is easy to learn and lots of fun to play. So, get out your chessboard, grab a partner, and play chess!

LET's Play

A Step-by-Step

Chess!

Guide for Beginners

BRUCE PANDOLFINI

WANDERER BOOKS
Published by Simon & Schuster, New York

Published by Wanderer Books
A Simon & Schuster Division of
Gulf & Western Corporation
Simon & Schuster Building
1230 Avenue of the Americas
New York, New York 10020

Designed by Irving Perkins

Manufactured in the United States of America

10 9 8 7 6 5 4 3 2 1

Wanderer and colophon are trademarks
of Simon & Schuster

Also available in Julian Messner Certified Edition

Library of Congress Cataloging in Publication Data

Pandolfini, Bruce.
Let's play chess!

Includes index.
SUMMARY: Presents chess fundamentals in numbered
statements in graded sequence with 198 diagrams.
1. Chess—Juvenile literature [1. Chess]
I. Title.
GV1446.P34   796.1'2   79-25966
ISBN 0-671-33061-6 pbk.

For Idelle

CONTENTS

Acknowledgments

I would like to thank Carol Ann Caronia for her careful reading of the manuscript and thoughtful suggestions; Idelle Pandolfini for her artwork and helpful improvements in expression; and Paul Hoffman of Scientific American for his ideas, rewriting, and logic. I also want to express gratitude to my two editors, Iris Rosoff and Bob Hernandez, for their understanding and valuable suggestions. The concern and editorial skills of these five have made possible *Let's Play Chess!*

Introduction

Chess is by far the most popular board game in the world. There are millions of players of all ages and the number grows every day. Maybe it's because you become a general who directs an army against your opponent in an exciting battle of wits. Whatever the reason, chess is challenging and a lot of fun as well.

You don't have to be a particular age to be a good player. Some young people have been known to play better chess than experienced adults. Bobby Fischer, the American chess genius, was beating adult international chess grandmasters before he was fifteen years old. The younger you are when you start playing, the better a chess player you'll be.

This is my attempt to lure you to the royal game. It is based on the very same lessons I have given to thousands of beginners. Their questions and problems have shaped it.

Moreover, some of the best ideas in the book were actually suggested by new players!

I have tried to be as direct as possible. To make your journey a smooth one, the fundamentals have been broken down into short, logical statements. Each idea is numbered, ordered, and clearly stated. For the most part, statements are linked in graded sequence with the easier ones preceding the harder. The format is unique and easy to follow. You should feel yourself learning step by step.

You will see how chess players think about their moves. Where desirable, explanation has replaced calculation. The stress is on understanding, not memory. There are plenty of diagrams for almost every idea. Except for one practice section, you can even read this book without a chess set!

How should you use *Let's Play Chess!*? To get the most from your efforts, start on page 15 and read each statement in numbered order. Try to cover entire sections in one reading. If a particular point seems confusing, read onward. You can always come back after you've thought about it and learned more. Besides, you can read this book and play chess without understanding every detail.

Now that you've made the first move, read on and start playing.

Let's Play Chess!

8	QR1 / QR8	QN1 / QN8	QB1 / QB8	Q1 / Q8	K1 / K8	KB1 / KB8	KN1 / KN8	KR1 / KR8	1
7	QR2 / QR7	QN2 / QN7	QB2 / QB7	Q2 / Q7	K2 / K7	KB2 / KB7	KN2 / KN7	KR2 / KR7	2
6	QR3 / QR6	QN3 / QN6	QB3 / QB6	Q3 / Q6	K3 / K6	KB3 / KB6	KN3 / KN6	KR3 / KR6	3
5	QR4 / QR5	QN4 / QN5	QB4 / QB5	Q4 / Q5	K4 / K5	KB4 / KB5	KN4 / KN5	KR4 / KR5	4
4	QR5 / QR4	QN5 / QN4	QB5 / QB4	Q5 / Q4	K5 / K4	KB5 / KB4	KN5 / KN4	KR5 / KR4	5
3	QR6 / QR3	QN6 / QN3	QB6 / QB3	Q6 / Q3	K6 / K3	KB6 / KB3	KN6 / KN3	KR6 / KR3	6
2	QR7 / QR2	QN7 / QN2	QB7 / QB2	Q7 / Q2	K7 / K2	KB7 / KB2	KN7 / KN2	KR7 / KR2	7
1	QR8 / QR1	QN8 / QN1	QB8 / QB1	Q8 / Q1	K8 / K1	KB8 / KB1	KN8 / KN1	KR8 / KR1	8

White

CHAPTER 1

GENERAL RULES

1. Chess is a game of skill played by two people on a board of sixty-four squares (the same board as used in checkers).

2. The squares of the chessboard are alternately colored light and dark to help the players see better.

3. The players, starting at opposite ends of the board, take turns by moving their own armies, one soldier on a turn.

4. Each *army* consists of sixteen soldiers called *chessmen*.

5. The lighter color army is always called *White* and the darker one *Black*, regardless of their actual colors.

6. In chess the players take turns to move. White moves first, then Black, then White, then Black, and so on.

7. Turns are taken by *moving* or *capturing*.

8. A *move* is the transfer of a chessman from one square to another.

9. Chessmen are placed in the middle of squares and not on their intersections.

10. A move can be legal or illegal.

11. A *legal move* abides by the rules of the game: it can be played. An *illegal move* violates the rules of the game: It cannot be played.

12. Illegal moves must be taken back and replayed.

13. A *capture* is a move that removes an enemy chessman from the board.

14. Chessmen are not jumped, as in checkers.

15. Unlike checkers, in chess you are not forced to capture enemy chessmen. Instead, it's a matter of choice.

16. Any chessman may capture any enemy chessman.

17. No move or capture *has* to be played, unless it's the only way to save the King from capture (more on this later).

18. You cannot—
    (a) capture your own chessmen,
    (b) place two chessmen on the same square,
    (c) move or capture two chessmen on a turn,
    (d) move a chessman in two different directions on the same turn (except for the Knight, which will be explained later).

THE BOARD, THE MEN, AND THEIR NAMES

19. The chessboard is the battlefield on which the two generals, you and your opponent, meet. It is a large

square made up of sixty-four smaller squares (there are eight rows of eight squares each).

DIAGRAM 1
The Chessboard

20. The smaller squares are arranged in three different kinds of rows.

 (a) **Horizontal rows**

 (b) **Vertical rows**

 (c) **Slanted rows**

21. The horizontal rows are *ranks*, the vertical rows are *files*, and the slanted rows are *diagonals*.

22. To explain the game of chess it is helpful to use diagrams. A *diagram* is a picture of a chess position in which symbols are used to represent the chessmen. For example, diagram 2 illustrates the opening position of a chess game.

DIAGRAM 2

23. For all diagrams in this book, unless otherwise indicated, White sits at the bottom and Black at the top. Consequently, the White Pawns move up the board and the Black move down.

Black's Pawns move   DIAGRAM 3

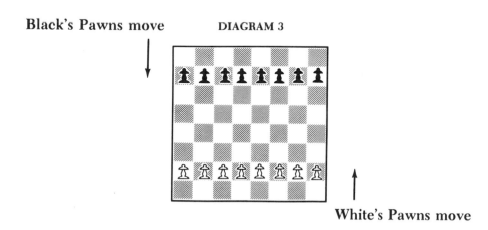

White's Pawns move

24. For both diagrams and real chess games each player must have a light square in the corner to his right.

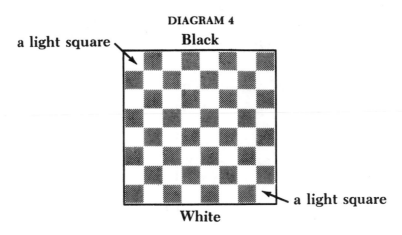

DIAGRAM 4

a light square

Black

a light square

White

25. Both you and your opponent start with an army of eight pieces and eight Pawns each.

	White	*Chessmen*	*Black*	*Abbreviation*
	♔	1 King	♚	K
	♕	1 Queen	♛	Q
	♖ ♖	2 Rooks	♜ ♜	R
	♗ ♗	2 Bishops	♝ ♝	B
	♘ ♘	2 Knights	♞ ♞	N
	♙ ♙ ♙ ♙ ♙ ♙ ♙ ♙	8 Pawns	♟ ♟ ♟ ♟ ♟ ♟ ♟ ♟	P

26. Notice that the Knight is abbreviated with an N, even though it begins with a K, to avoid confusion with the abbreviation for King.

27. Chessmen are referred to as *pieces* and Pawns. You may call any chessman a piece, except for the Pawn.

28. In the beginning, your pieces occupy the rank closest to you and your Pawns occupy the next rank in.

29. From opposite sides of the chessboard, the same kinds of White and Black pieces occupy squares directly across from each other. Along the same files, Rooks oppose Rooks, Knights oppose Knights, and so on.

DIAGRAM 5

The same kinds of pieces face each other

30. In setting up the pieces, you might confuse the squares occupied by the Queen and King. There is an easy way to avoid this confusion: Queens always start on squares of their own color.

31.   At the start, White's Queen occupies a light square and Black's a dark one (this is true only if you start correctly with a light square in the corner to your right).

32.   Remember: Queen on her own color.

The Black Queen occupies a dark square

DIAGRAM 6

The Queen goes on the square of her own color

The White Queen occupies a light square

33.   Every square and piece on the chessboard has a specific name. You will find this book far easier if you learn these names right away.

34.   The board is divided in half, into the *Kingside* and the *Queenside*.

35.   The Rooks, Bishops, and Knights are named according to which side of the board they are on at the start of the game. Moving across the board from left to right, there is the Queen Rook, the Queen Knight,

the Queen Bishop, the Queen, the King, the King
Bishop, the King Knight, and the King Rook.

DIAGRAM 7

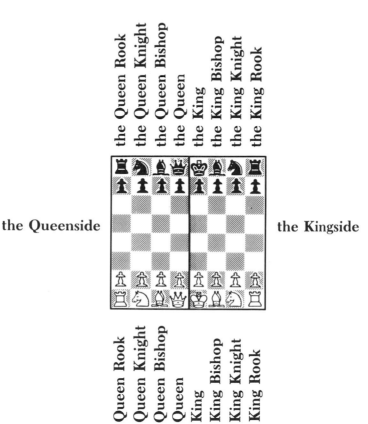

the Queenside   the Kingside

36.   The name of a piece never changes, no matter where
it is moved. The King Rook is always the King Rook,
even if it winds up on the Queenside.

37. Files receive their names from the pieces that occupy them at the start of play. In the beginning, the file containing the Queen Rook is the Queen Rook file, the file containing the King Bishop is the King Bishop file, and so on.

DIAGRAM 8

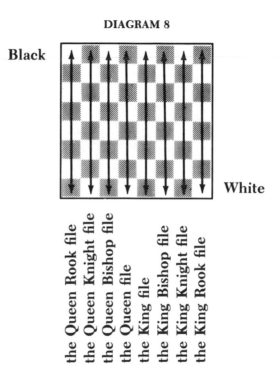

Black

White

the Queen Rook file
the Queen Knight file
the Queen Bishop file
the Queen file
the King file
the King Bishop file
the King Knight file
the King Rook file

38. The name of a file never changes, no matter what happens to the piece that originally occupies it.

39. Ranks are numbered according to your point of view on the board. You look at the board either from the White side or the Black side.

40. Proceeding from the White side and moving toward
     the Black, there is the first rank, second rank, third
     rank, fourth rank, fifth rank, sixth rank, seventh rank,
     and eighth rank.

41. Since Black looks at the board in the opposite way,
     White's first rank is Black's eighth rank, White's sec-
     ond rank is Black's seventh rank, White's third rank
     is Black's sixth rank, and so on.

DIAGRAM 9

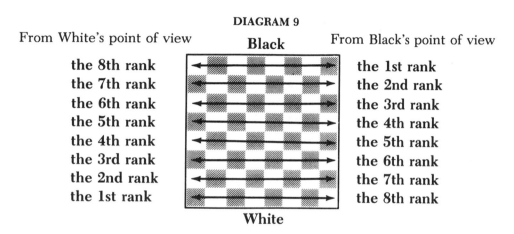

From White's point of view	Black	From Black's point of view
the 8th rank		the 1st rank
the 7th rank		the 2nd rank
the 6th rank		the 3rd rank
the 5th rank		the 4th rank
the 4th rank		the 5th rank
the 3rd rank		the 6th rank
the 2nd rank		the 7th rank
the 1st rank		the 8th rank

White

42. To name a square, combine the name of the file with
     the number of the rank. Every square has two names
     because there are two points of view. (If the point of
     view is not indicated, assume it is White).

43. The following diagram names the squares from both
     points of view. The names are abbreviated (for exam-
     ple, King Knight 7 is written KN7) and the Black
     names are given upside down.

8	QR8	QN8	QB8	Q8	K8	KB8	KN8	KR8
7	QR7	QN7	QB7	Q7	K7	KB7	KN7	KR7
6	QR6	QN6	QB6	Q6	K6	KB6	KN6	KR6
5	QR5	QN5	QB5	Q5	K5	KB5	KN5	KR5
4	QR4	QN4	QB4	Q4	K4	KB4	KN4	KR4
3	QR3	QN3	QB3	Q3	K3	KB3	KN3	KR3
2	QR2	QN2	QB2	Q2	K2	KB2	KN2	KR2
1	QR1	QN1	QB1	Q1	K1	KB1	KN1	KR1

(Right-side rank numbers, top to bottom: 1, 2, 3, 4, 5, 6, 7, 8. Each square also bears the inverted Black-perspective label.)

White

44. Pawns take their names from the files they occupy at any given time. A Pawn on the Queen Rook file is a Queen Rook Pawn (abbreviated QRP).

DIAGRAM 10

Black

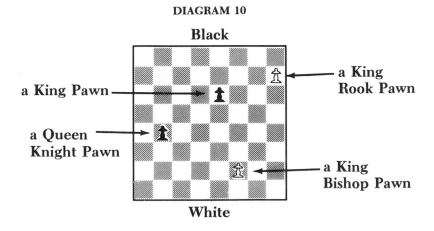

a King Pawn

a King Rook Pawn

a Queen Knight Pawn

a King Bishop Pawn

White

45. Groups of squares can be referred to by their color. Regardless of their actual colors, the thirty-two darker squares are called the dark squares and the thirty-two lighter squares are called the light squares.

46. Remember that squares are light and dark, but chessmen are White and Black.

47. Now you should be able to refer to any part of the board or to any kind of chessman accurately.

THE MOVES OF THE PIECES

 The King

48. The King is usually the tallest and always the most important piece, though its significance will not become clear until later.

49. The King moves just one square at a time in any direction.

50. In diagram 11, the King can move to any square marked by a dot on one turn.

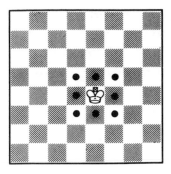

DIAGRAM 11
The King's Move

To any square marked by a dot

51. The King captures by moving as it would normally, and then replacing the enemy chessman that occupies the square it lands on.

52. In diagrams 12 and 13 the White King captures the Black Pawn (on this move it could also capture the Black Knight, but not the Black Rook).

DIAGRAMS 12 AND 13
How the King Captures

Before   After

White may capture either the Knight or Pawn

White has captured the Pawn

 **The Rook**

53. The Rook is the piece mistakenly called the Castle.

54. The Rook moves along ranks and files (forward, backward, or sideways) as many unblocked squares as desired.

55. It can move in only one direction on a turn (whichever one you choose).

56. In diagram 14 the Rook can move to any square marked by a dot.

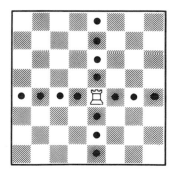

DIAGRAM 14
The Rook's Move

To any square marked by a dot

57. A Rook captures by moving in its normal way, and then replacing the enemy chessman that occupies the square it lands on.

58. In diagrams 15 and 16 the White Rook captures the Black Bishop (it could also have captured the Knight).

DIAGRAMS 15 AND 16
How the Rook Captures

Before   After

White may capture
either the Knight or
Bishop

The Rook has captured
the Bishop

59. Rooks cannot—

(a) take their own chessmen,
(b) move to squares occupied by their own men,
(c) jump over enemy or friendly chessmen,
(d) capture two or more enemy chessmen on the same turn,
(e) move diagonally.

 The Bishop

60. Bishops move only on diagonals (the slanted rows of one color) as many unblocked squares as desired.

61. They can move backward or forward, but only in one direction on a turn.

62. In diagram 17 the White Bishop can move to any square marked by a dot.

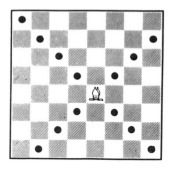

DIAGRAM 17
The Bishop's Move

To any square marked by a dot

63. A Bishop captures by moving in its normal way, and then replacing the enemy chessman that occupies the square it lands on.

64. In diagrams 18 and 19 the White Bishop captures the Black Bishop.

DIAGRAMS 18 AND 19
How the Bishop Captures

Before

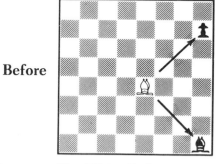

After

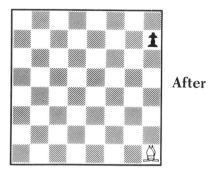

The White Bishop may capture either the Black Pawn or Bishop

White has captured the Bishop

65. Each side starts with both a light square and a dark square Bishop. The *light square* Bishop travels only on light squares, while the *dark square* Bishop travels only on dark squares (this is determined by the color of the square the Bishop occupies at the start of the game).

66. Bishops cannot—

    (a) capture two or more enemy chessmen on a turn,
    (b) capture their own chessmen,
    (c) jump over enemy or friendly chessmen,
    (d) move to a square occupied by one of their own men,
    (e) move along ranks and files.

67. How many moves would it take for a Bishop starting on White's QB1 to reach White's QR6?

DIAGRAM 20

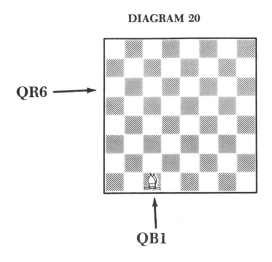

QR6

QB1

68. Answer: none. It can't be done! A dark square Bishop can never move to a light square (nor can a light square Bishop move to a dark square).

69. During the course of a game a Bishop can occupy no more than thirty-two different squares on the board (compare this to a Rook, which is capable of reaching every square).

 The Queen

70. The Queen is the most powerful piece of all.

71. The Queen combines the movements of the Rook and Bishop (which means it functions as both Rook and Bishop).

72. The Queen moves in any direction (forward, backward, sideways, or diagonally) as many unblocked squares as desired.

73. In diagram 21 the Queen can move to any square marked by a dot.

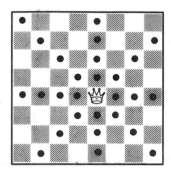

DIAGRAM 21
The Queen's Move

To any square marked by a dot

74. The Queen captures by moving in its normal way, and then replacing the enemy chessman that occupies the square it lands on.

75. In diagram 22 the White Queen can capture any of the circled Black chessmen, but only one on a turn.

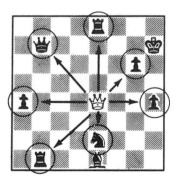

DIAGRAM 22
The Queen's Capture

76. The Queen cannot—

   (a) capture its own chessmen,
   (b) jump over enemy or friendly chessmen,
   (c) move to a square occupied by one of its own chessmen,

(d) capture two or more enemy chessmen on the same turn.

 The Knight

77. The Knight is the piece mistakenly called the Horse.

78. Its movement is the most difficult to learn because it has two different parts. Both parts together, however, are to be viewed as one complete turn.

79. The Knight can move in any direction, but it must always make a move of the same length.

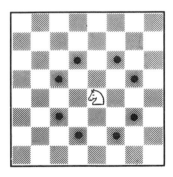

DIAGRAM 23
The Knight's Move

To any square marked by a dot

80. The Knight's move looks like the capital letter **L**.

81. Before describing it further, let's examine it. In diagram 23 the White Knight can move to any square marked by a dot. Notice that the dots seem to form a circle around the Knight.

82. There are many different ways to describe the Knight's movement. We shall examine four of them.

83. The Knight can move:

(a) Two squares vertically then one square horizontally

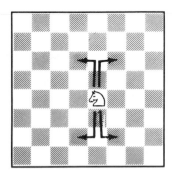

DIAGRAMS 24–27
The Knight's Move

Diagrams 24 and 25 outline the same moves

(b) One square horizontally then two squares vertically

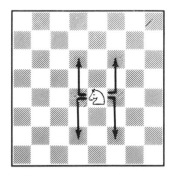

(c)   Two squares horizontally then one square vertically

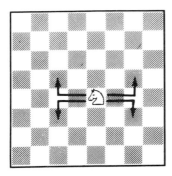

Diagrams 26 and 27 outline the same moves

(d)   One square vertically then two squares horizontally

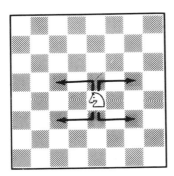

84.   Notice that 83a and 83b describe one set of Knight moves, while 83c and 83d describe another set of Knight moves.

85. Thus, by the system in 83a–d, each Knight move can be described in at least two ways.

86. At this point you should practice moving the Knight. The following diagram shows a sequence of 8 Knight moves. Study it very carefully and try to trace the same 8 moves on your own board.

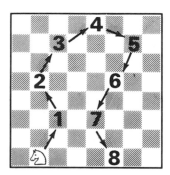

DIAGRAM 28
Eight Knight Moves

Each number in succession represents the next Knight move

87. Knights are the only pieces that can jump over other chessmen. (The only way they can be blocked is if all squares to which they can be moved are occupied by their own men.)

88. In diagram 29 the White Knight can move to any of the squares marked by a dot even though there are both friendly and enemy pieces in the way. Notice that the Knight still traces an **L**, as if the blocking pieces didn't exist.

DIAGRAM 29

The Knight can jump over any
chessman
White's Knight can move to any
square marked by a dot

89. Knights are the only pieces capable of moving in the
opening position (all the others are blocked by Pawns
—see diagram 2).

90. A Knight captures by moving in its normal way, and
then replacing the enemy chessman that occupies
the square it lands on.

91. In diagrams 30 and 31 the White Knight captures the
Black Rook.

DIAGRAMS 30 AND 31
The Knight's Capture

Before 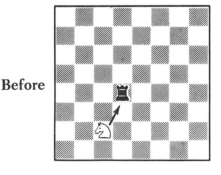  After

92. The Knight is the only piece that, from move to move, must change the color of the square it occupies. Test this out by moving the Knight across the board for a few moves.

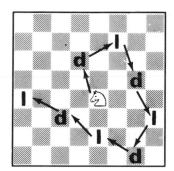

DIAGRAM 32

The Knight moves to a different color square from the one it occupies (d=dark square/l=light square)

Exercise for the Knight's Move

93. For this exercise, all squares are named from the White side. On an empty board place a White Knight on QR1 (don't try to do this in your head). From QR1 maneuver the Knight to QN1. This takes 3 moves. One way to do it is to play the Knight from QR1 to QN3, then from there to Q2, then from there to QN1. Diagram 33 illustrates this.

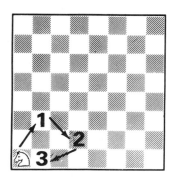

DIAGRAMS 33–36
*Four Ways to Move the Knight
(Follow the Arrows)*

From QR1 to QN1

94. Another way to do it is to move the Knight from QR1 to QB2, then from there to QR3, then from there to QN1. Mission accomplished. Diagram 34 illustrates this other way.

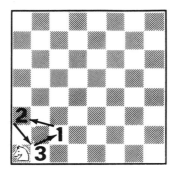

From QR1 to QN1

95. Then with the same kind of three-step maneuver, move the Knight from QN1 to QB1. This could be done, for example, by moving the Knight from QN1 to QB3 to K2 to QB1.

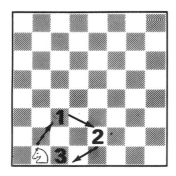

From QN1 to QB1

96. Then from QB1, maneuver the Knight to Q1, then to K1, and so on, until you have maneuvered the

Knight entirely across White's first rank—stopping at each successive square along the rank every 3 moves.

97. From KR1 then maneuver the Knight to KR2. Again it takes 3 moves. One way to do it, for example, is to play the Knight from KR1 to KN3 to KB1 to KR2. Diagram 36 illustrates this maneuver.

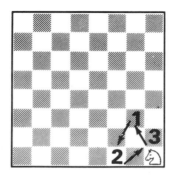

From KR1 to KR2

98. From KR2 work the Knight across the second rank, in the same way you worked it across the first rank, until the Knight reaches the square QR2.

99. Then from QR2 maneuver the Knight to QR3—it again takes 3 moves. From QR3, covering every square on the third rank, work the Knight across to KR3.

100. Use this procedure to maneuver the Knight around the entire board, stopping every 3 moves on the next

square in succession, until each square on the board has been occupied.

101. Try this exercise every day and time it. The faster you complete the *Knight's tour*, as it is called, the better your grasp of the Knight's movement. In addition, this exercise gives practice thinking 3 moves ahead, and thinking ahead is one of the best things a chess player can do.

102. A Knight cannot—

(a) capture its own chessmen,
(b) move to a square occupied by one of its own chessmen,
(c) capture two or more enemy chessmen on the same turn.

REVIEW CHART OF HOW THE PIECES MOVE

PIECE	HOW IT MOVES
Rook	along ranks and files from one to seven squares per move
Bishop	along diagonals from one to seven squares per move
Queen	along ranks, files, and diagonals from one to seven squares per move
King	along ranks, files, and diagonals but only one square per move
Knight	like an **L** in any direction

The Strange World of Pawns

103. I refer to Pawns as being strange because they are truly different from all other chessmen.

104. Pawns are the foot soldiers—the infantrymen—of chess. Essentially very weak, they can become very powerful as they advance up the board.

105. Pawns move straight ahead, one square on a turn (vertically up the board for White, and vertically down the board for Black).

106. In diagram 37 White may move his Pawn to the square marked by the arrow.

DIAGRAM 37
The Pawn's Move

White's Pawn on QB3 can move to QB4

107. Pawns cannot move backward. (They are the only chessmen that can't.)

108. There is a special rule that applies to each Pawn's first move. On the first move, you have the option of moving it either one or two squares.

109. Thus, in diagram 38, White can move his Pawn to either Q3 or Q4.

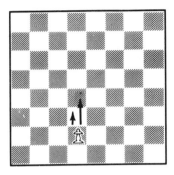

DIAGRAM 38
The Pawn's Two-Square Option

110. Once a Pawn has moved, however, you lose the right to move it two squares. This is so even if the Pawn did not move two squares on its first move.

111. Therefore, in diagram 39, since it will be the Pawn's second move, the White Pawn can only move to K4 and not K5.

DIAGRAM 39

112.   Pawns are the only chessmen that capture differently from the way they move. They capture one square diagonally ahead.

113.   Thus, in diagrams 40 and 41, the White Pawn captures the Black Bishop.

DIAGRAMS 40–41
The Pawn's Capture

Before  After

White's Pawn may
capture either the
Bishop or Knight

White's Pawn has
captured the Bishop

114.   Pawns cannot capture one square vertically ahead.

115.   Pawns cannot capture two squares diagonally ahead. The two-square option does not apply to captures.

116.   Thus, in diagram 42, White's Pawn cannot take Black's even though White's Pawn has not yet moved.

DIAGRAM 42

White cannot capture Black's Pawn

117. Pawns cannot capture backward.

118. Pawns cannot move or capture horizontally.

119. At the start of the game each side has eight Pawns on its second rank. Therefore, the Pawns block and prevent the pieces from coming out (except for the Knights, which can jump over anything).

120. For now, this is all you have to know about Pawns. Later on you will learn of special rules that apply to these miniature foot soldiers.

THE OBJECT OF THE GAME

121. Now that you have learned how the chessmen move, you must learn what to do with them.

122. The object of a chess game is to capture the enemy King.

123. Here for the first time we encounter the two most often heard chess terms: *Checkmate* and *check*. (*Checkmate* will be shortened to *mate* for the remainder of the book.)

124. Before proceeding, it is helpful to remember that a chessman is *attacked* when it is threatened by capture.

125. You are *in check* when your King is placed under direct attack by an enemy chessman. You *give check* when one of your own chessmen attacks the opposing King directly.

126. Diagram 43 shows the White King in check from the Black Bishop.

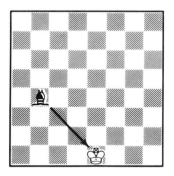

DIAGRAM 43

Check

127. Since losing the King entails losing the game, a player whose King is placed in check must get it out of check.

128.   There are three different ways to get out of check:

(a)   By blocking the enemy attacker (by putting a chessman in the way)
(b)   By capturing the enemy attacker
(c)   By moving your King

129.   Diagrams 44–47 show Black giving check and the three different ways to get out of check.

DIAGRAMS 44–47
The Three Ways to Get Out of Check

Black is giving check. White can get out of check by:

(a) blocking the Bishop by moving the Pawn to QB3

(b) capturing the Bishop with the Rook

(c) moving the King to K2 and out of the Bishop's line of attack

130. If all three ways to get out of check are possible, you may choose any one of the three (you may either block, capture, or move away).

131. It is illegal—

   (a) to move into check,
   (b) not to get out of check when it is possible,
   (c) to capture a King that illegally moves into check (instead, the illegal King move must be re-played),
   (d) to capture a King that could have, but didn't get out of check (the enemy must be given a chance to replay the move).

132. Suppose your King is suddenly checked and there is no way to prevent its capture on the next move. What then?

133. If you are unable to avoid capture of your King on the next move, the game is over—you have been *mated*.

134. Diagram 48 illustrates *mate*.

DIAGRAM 48

Mate

135. In diagram 48 White is unable to block the Bishop's check, capture the Bishop, or move his King to a *safe square* (a square not guarded by enemy chessmen). White has been mated by Black.

136. The game is over as soon as mate is given. You do not actually capture the enemy King.

137. To get a feeling for mate, diagrams 49–52 show you the shortest game possible: Black mates White in 2 moves. This is called the *fool's mate*.

DIAGRAMS 49–52

White's first move: **Pawn to KB3**

Black's first move: **Pawn to K4**

White's second move: **Pawn to KN4**

Black's second move: **Queen to KR5 mate!**

138.   It is mate because—

    (a)   the White King is in check from the Black Queen,

    (b)   the White King cannot escape to a safe square,

    (c)   no White chessman can block the check,

    (d)   the Black Queen cannot be captured,

    (e)   the White King will be captured next move.

139.   Remember:

    (a)   Check occurs when the King is attacked but its capture can be avoided on the next move

(b) Mate occurs when the King is attacked and its capture cannot be avoided on the next move

140. Beginners mistakenly think that check must be announced. Some players even announce check to the Queen. There are no such rules. Besides, saying "check" may actually disturb your opponent, causing him to lose his concentration.

141. There are two ways to lose a chess game:

(a) By mate
(b) By *resignation* (by giving up)

142. Most players prefer resigning to being mated. This is true especially for advanced players. In order to become a winner, however, you must lose many times. There is a chess saying that no one ever won a game by resigning.

	QR	QN	QB	Q	K	KB	KN	KR	
8	QR1 / QR8	QN1 / QN8	QB1 / QB8	Q1 / Q8	K1 / K8	KB1 / KB8	KN1 / KN8	KR1 / KR8	**1**
7	QR2 / QR7	QN2 / QN7	QB2 / QB7	Q2 / Q7	K2 / K7	KB2 / KB7	KN2 / KN7	KR2 / KR7	**2**
6	QR3 / QR6	QN3 / QN6	QB3 / QB6	Q3 / Q6	K3 / K6	KB3 / KB6	KN3 / KN6	KR3 / KR6	**3**
5	QR4 / QR5	QN4 / QN5	QB4 / QB5	Q4 / Q5	K4 / K5	KB4 / KB5	KN4 / KN5	KR4 / KR5	**4**
4	QR5 / QR4	QN5 / QN4	QB5 / QB4	Q5 / Q4	K5 / K4	KB5 / KB4	KN5 / KN4	KR5 / KR4	**5**
3	QR6 / QR3	QN6 / QN3	QB6 / QB3	Q6 / Q3	K6 / K3	KB6 / KB3	KN6 / KN3	KR6 / KR3	**6**
2	QR7 / QR2	QN7 / QN2	QB7 / QB2	Q7 / Q2	K7 / K2	KB7 / KB2	KN7 / KN2	KR7 / KR2	**7**
1	QR8 / QR1	QN8 / QN1	QB8 / QB1	Q8 / Q1	K8 / K1	KB8 / KB1	KN8 / KN1	KR8 / KR1	**8**

White

CHAPTER 2

MATING PATTERNS

143. In chess, it is necessary to play with a goal in mind. There should be a reason behind every move.

144. The ultimate goal of chess is to mate the enemy King.

145. Usually, a few chessmen are needed to give mate. One chessman checks the enemy King, while others keep it from escaping.

146. A successful chess player has a stockpile of mating patterns.

147. A *mating pattern* is a mate given by one or more chessmen in a particular way or in a definite formation. There are hundreds of different mating patterns.

148. Diagram 53 shows a mating pattern involving the Queen and Bishop. Examine the position carefully and make sure that the Black King cannot avoid being captured on the next move.

149. Remember that the King is never allowed to move into check.

DIAGRAM 53

150. It is mate because—

(a) the White Bishop checks the Black King,
(b) the White Bishop cannot be blocked or captured,

(c) the Black King has no safe escape square,

(d) the Black King is going to be captured on White's next move.

151. In diagram 54 try to find how White can mate Black in one move. Hint: In all problems of this kind, start by looking for moves that check the enemy King.

DIAGRAM 54

152. The solution is **Q × BP mate**. (This is read: Queen takes Bishop Pawn mate—since only the King Bishop Pawn and not the Queen Bishop Pawn can be captured by the White Queen, you don't have to say Q × KBP—you can drop the K).

DIAGRAM 55

153. It is mate because—

   (a) the White Queen checks the Black King,
   (b) the White Queen cannot be captured legally (it is protected by the White Bishop on QB4),
   (c) the White Queen cannot be blocked,
   (d) there are no escape squares for the Black King,
   (e) the Black King is going to be captured on the next move.

154. In diagram 56 White can mate Black in 1 move. Find the move.

DIAGRAM 56

155. The solution is **R–R8 mate**. (This is read: Rook to Rook 8 mate.)

DIAGRAM 57

156. It is mate because—

> (a) the White Rook checks the Black King,
> (b) the White Rook cannot be captured legally (it is protected by the White Bishop on KR1),
> (c) the White Rook cannot be blocked,
> (d) all the squares the Black King could move to are guarded by White (the White Rook guards QR7 and QB8 while the White Bishop guards QN7),
> (e) the Black King is going to be captured on the next move.

Just a reminder: It is not mate if the checking chessman can be captured, if the check can be blocked, or if the defending King can move away.

TWENTY MATING PATTERNS

157. Diagrams 58-77 (the next twenty pairs of diagrams) show some common mating patterns. Cover the answer diagram on the right and figure out which chessman can be moved in the diagram on the left to mate the Black King. Study the diagrams closely— they show how chessmen work together to give mate. Notice that chessmen not directly involved in the mating patterns are not shown, which is why the White King is sometimes absent.

DIAGRAM 58

Solution: the Rook mates

DIAGRAM 59

Solution: the Queen mates

DIAGRAM 60

Solution: the Knight mates

DIAGRAM 61

Solution: the Queen mates

DIAGRAM 62

Solution: the Queen mates

DIAGRAM 63

Solution: the Knight on
QB2 mates

Mating Patterns 61

DIAGRAM 64

Solution: the Bishop
mates

DIAGRAM 65

Solution: the light
square Bishop mates

DIAGRAM 66

Solution: the Rook on
K1 mates

DIAGRAM 67

Solution: the Rook on
KN7 mates

DIAGRAM 68

Solution: the Queen
mates

DIAGRAM 69

Solution: the Queen
mates

Mating Patterns 63

DIAGRAM 70

Solution: the Rook mates

DIAGRAM 71

Solution: the Pawn on QB7 mates

DIAGRAM 72

Solution: the Knight mates

DIAGRAM 73

Solution: the Rook mates

DIAGRAM 74

Solution: the Bishop mates

DIAGRAM 75

Solution: the Knight mates

Mating Patterns   65

DIAGRAM 76

Solution: the Knight
mates

DIAGRAM 77

Solution: the light
square Bishop mates

158. Mating problems to be solved in 1 move are seldom difficult, but mating problems to be solved in 2 or more moves often are.

159. Mating problems are described in specific ways. "White to play and mate in 2 moves" means that White plays a move, Black responds, and then White

gives mate. To put it another way, White plays 2 moves and Black plays 1 move.

160. "Black to play and mate in 2 moves" means that Black plays a move, White responds, and then Black gives mate. In other words, Black plays 2 moves and White plays 1 move.

161. Some problems in chess books require that you look further ahead than 2 moves. Trying to look ahead creates a problem: how can you see your opponent's responses? You know what you're going to play, but how can you determine what he's going to play?

162. The difficulty of a chess problem depends on the number of possible enemy responses. The more enemy responses, the more difficult the problem is.

163. The easiest problems to solve are those that force the enemy to respond with a particular move.

164. The strongest moves are *threats* to capture chessmen (they should be answered) and the most serious threats are checks (they must be answered).

165. When considering a mating problem, try to find moves (such as checks) that force particular responses.

166. The next problem allows the defender only one possible response to the correct first move (hint: look for a check). It is not as hard as you might first think.

167. Diagram 78 illustrates a position where White can play and mate Black in 2 moves. Try to solve the problem, but don't be alarmed if you have difficulty. The ability to look ahead comes with experience.

168. Remember: Start your investigation by looking for checks.

DIAGRAM 78

169. White's correct first move is **R–K8ch**. (This is read: Rook to King 8 check.)

DIAGRAM 79

170. Black's only possible response is to capture the White Rook with his Rook: **R × R**. (This is read: Rook takes Rook.)

DIAGRAM 80

171. On his second move, White captures the Black Rook and gives mate: **R × R mate**.

DIAGRAM 81

172. It is mate because—

    (a) the White Rook checks the Black King,
    (b) the White Rook cannot be captured or blocked,
    (c) the Black King cannot escape (get out of check),
    (d) the Black King will be captured on the next move.

173.   Review this section carefully. If you have trouble
       with it, go on. For now it is enough that you have
       been introduced to mating patterns. You can worry
       about mastering them later.

       An old Chinese proverb says that a journey of a thou-
       sand miles begins with a single step.

	QR	QN	QB	Q	K	KB	KN	KR	
8	QR1 / QR8	QN1 / QN8	QB1 / QB8	Q1 / Q8	K1 / K8	KB1 / KB8	KN1 / KN8	KR1 / KR8	1
7	QR2 / QR7	QN2 / QN7	QB2 / QB7	Q2 / Q7	K2 / K7	KB2 / KB7	KN2 / KN7	KR2 / KR7	2
6	QR3 / QR6	QN3 / QN6	QB3 / QB6	Q3 / Q6	K3 / K6	KB3 / KB6	KN3 / KN6	KR3 / KR6	3
5	QR4 / QR5	QN4 / QN5	QB4 / QB5	Q4 / Q5	K4 / K5	KB4 / KB5	KN4 / KN5	KR4 / KR5	4
4	QR5 / QR4	QN5 / QN4	QB5 / QB4	Q5 / Q4	K5 / K4	KB5 / KB4	KN5 / KN4	KR5 / KR4	5
3	QR6 / QR3	QN6 / QN3	QB6 / QB3	Q6 / Q3	K6 / K3	KB6 / KB3	KN6 / KN3	KR6 / KR3	6
2	QR7 / QR2	QN7 / QN2	QB7 / QB2	Q7 / Q2	K7 / K2	KB7 / KB2	KN7 / KN2	KR7 / KR2	7
1	QR8 / QR1	QN8 / QN1	QB8 / QB1	Q8 / Q1	K8 / K1	KB8 / KB1	KN8 / KN1	KR8 / KR1	8

White

CHAPTER 3

Special Rules

CASTLING

174. Because the King is so vulnerable, chess has a special rule to help protect it (just as football has its special rule to help protect the quarterback).

175.   This special rule is called *castling*, and it is the only
        time during a game that two pieces can be moved on
        the same turn.

176.   In diagram 82 the squares on the first rank, between
        the King and King Rook, are unoccupied. If both the
        King and King Rook have not yet moved in the
        game, then White may castle.

DIAGRAM 82

177.   Castling is done by moving the King two squares
        toward the Rook (in this case to KN1) and then mov-
        ing the Rook to the other side of the King (in this case
        to KB1). This is illustrated by diagrams 83–85.

DIAGRAMS 83–85
How to Castle

Before

After

178. The kind of castling in diagrams 83–85 is called *castling Kingside*. There are two kinds of castling:

(a) Castling Kingside
(b) Castling Queenside

179. In diagrams 86 and 87 White castles Queenside (assuming neither the King nor Rook has moved) by moving the King two squares toward the Rook (in this case to QB1) and then moving the Rook to the other side of the King (in this case to Q1).

DIAGRAMS 86–87
Castling Queenside

Before

After

180. Diagrams 88–90 show Kingside and Queenside castling for Black.

DIAGRAMS 88–90
Castling for Black

Before

After castling Kingside   After castling Queenside

181. Both White and Black are allowed to castle just once during a game. Usually both sides exercise their castling rights.

182. Kingside castling happens more frequently than Queenside castling, mainly because it is easier and requires less effort (there is one less piece to get out of the way).

183. There are three additional factors that would make castling impossible:

   (a) If the castling King is already in check
   (b) If the castling King moves into check
   (c) If the castling King must pass through check (over a square guarded by the enemy)

184. In diagram 91 White cannot castle because his King is in check. If the checking Rook could be blocked, captured, or driven away, then White could castle on the next move or any other move after that.

DIAGRAM 91

White cannot castle while in check

185. In diagram 92 White cannot castle because he would be castling into check. If somehow the Black Bishop that guards KN1 could be driven away, blocked, or captured, then afterward White would still be able to castle Kingside.

DIAGRAM 92

You cannot castle into check

186. In order to castle in diagram 93 the White King would have to pass through check (over a square guarded by the Black Rook). Even though the King

doesn't stop on **KB1** (the square guarded by the Rook), White is unable to castle. If somehow the Black Rook could be blocked, driven away, or captured, then afterward White still could castle Kingside.

DIAGRAM 93

You cannot castle through check

187. Remember that the King is never allowed to move into check—it's against the rules.

188. Castling may happen at any time during the game, assuming it's a legal move.

189. To summarize, you cannot castle if—

    (a) King or Rook has moved,
    (b) the squares in between are blocked,
    (c) you've castled earlier,
    (d) you're in check,
    (e) you would have to move into check,
    (f) you would have to move through check.

DRAWING A CHESS GAME

190. It is possible for a chess game to end without anyone winning or losing. Games that end in this way are called *draws*.

191. Draws in chess are similar to ties in sports but are also somewhat different. Ties in sports usually require that both sides have the same score; draws in chess do not require that both sides have the same score (that is, the same number and kind of chessmen). In chess, it is possible to be far behind in *material* (another name for chessmen taken as a group) and still draw the game.

192. There are five different ways to draw a chess game:
    (a) Stalemate
    (b) The 50-move rule
    (c) Insufficient mating material
    (d) Threefold repetition
    (e) Agreement

Stalemate

193. If the side whose turn it is to play has no legal move and is not in check, then the game is drawn by stalemate.

194. If one side has been stalemated, the other has given the stalemate.

195. Diagrams 94–96 illustrate the concept of stalemate. In each case, it is Black's turn, and he has no legal move.

DIAGRAMS 94–96
Three Examples of Stalemate

Black is not in check and White's Queen guards all of the Black King's escape squares

Neither the Black King nor Pawn can move

All of the Black King's escape squares are guarded and Black is not in check

196. In diagram 96 White is far ahead in chessmen, but it does not matter—the game is still drawn by stalemate.

197.   This possibility of drawing a game when hopelessly behind in material is why most beginners stick it out to the very last man. Not surprisingly, some very famous chess games have ended in this way. (Sammy Reshevsky, one of the greatest players of all time, twice has fallen into stalemates during master competition).

The 50-Move Rule

198.   If 50 moves have been played without either a piece being captured *or* a Pawn being moved, then the player whose turn it is may claim a draw.

199.   If the above two conditions are fulfilled, a draw can be claimed regardless of all other circumstances on the board (with the exception that you can no longer claim a draw if you've been mated).

200.   Some amateurs mistakenly think that the 50-move rule is really a 15-, 16-, or 21-move rule. There are no such shortcuts.

201.   The 50-move rule is seldom used because it is easy to get around. For example, let's say 40 moves have been played and counted. In 10 more moves, the side that desires a draw can claim a draw. If anyone moves a Pawn or captures a chessman, however, the count must start all over again. Even as late as move

49 you still could be forced to start the count all over if either a Pawn is moved or a capture is made. To draw by the 50-move rule, your best chance lies in the attacker not knowing the rule at all.

Insufficient Mating Material

202.   A draw also can be claimed if neither side has enough material left to force mate. For example, a lone King cannot mate a lone King, for neither side can move into check. (While a King can protect a chessman that gives mate, it cannot give mate itself.)

203.   It is confusing to say, "A King can't take a King." This may cause you to think mistakenly that a King is allowed to move into check from another King. A King may never move into check from any chessman, including the opposing King.

204.   Two other examples of drawing by insufficient mating material:

(a)   One side has only a King and Bishop, and the other only a King
(b)   One side has only a King and Knight, and the other only a King

Test this out on a chessboard. You won't even be able to set up a mate, let alone force mate through playing.

Threefold Repetition

205. If the exact position occurs three or more times during a chess game, the player whose turn it is may claim a draw by the threefold repetition rule.

206. The repetitions need not occur on consecutive moves. They may happen at any points during the game.

207. A position is not really repeated unless every single detail is the same. Every chessman must be on the same square, the same player must be on the move, and so on. Don't think that a draw can be claimed if merely the same move is repeated three times.

208. If all requirements are fulfilled, the draw may be claimed by the player who is about to repeat the position for the third time, just before he does it.

209. It must be your turn in order to claim a draw by a threefold repetition. Don't make your move and then claim it. Once you've moved, it's already your opponent's turn and it's too late to claim a draw.

Agreement

210. The most common way to draw a game is for one side to propose a draw and for the other to accept. At least 95 percent of real draws arise in this way.

211. The correct way to offer a draw (as opposed to *claiming* a draw by the threefold repetition rule) is to make your move and then propose the draw.

PAWN PROMOTION

212. Pawns are the only chessmen that can change into other chessmen.

213. Because Pawns cannot go backward, it would seem that once a Pawn reaches its eighth rank it has nowhere to go. The rule of Pawn promotion, however, changes the whole picture.

214. When a Pawn reaches its last rank, it is promoted. This means it must be changed into a piece (either a Knight, Bishop, Rook, or Queen).

215. Diagrams 97–99 show a promotion sequence (before, during, and after).

White's turn to play

White moves his Pawn
to its eighth rank

and exchanges it for a
Queen

216. Since most players are likely to promote to a Queen, the most powerful piece, Pawn promotion is commonly referred to as "Queening a Pawn."

217. This possibility of a Pawn's transformation into a Queen is often the winning factor in a chess game (more on that later).

218.   Each Pawn upon reaching its eighth rank may be promoted, regardless of how many Pawns have already been promoted for either side.

219.   Consequently, it is possible for both White and Black to make as many as eight new pieces, of any kind or in any ratio. (The only exception is that you can't make a new King.) If somehow all eight Pawns sneak through, you can make as many as eight new Queens, or Knights, or Bishops, or Rooks (or any combination of these four pieces adding up to eight).

Can you imagine what it's like to be a Pawn? It's Clark Kent for the entire game, and then reaches the last rank and becomes Superman!

220.   Some beginners think that it is illegal to have two or more Bishops of the same color (Bishops that travel on squares of the same color). They are wrong—there is no such restriction.

221.   A piece made through promotion has the same powers as a natural one. A promoted Knight is identical to a natural Knight, a promoted Bishop is identical to a natural Bishop, and so on.

222.   As soon as a Pawn is moved to its eighth rank, it must be promoted. If an extra Queen is not available—or any other piece of your choosing—state what piece you want the Pawn to become and tie a rubberband

around it. (Otherwise you might confuse the promoted Pawn with just a plain Pawn.) Some players prefer using an upside-down Rook instead of the rubberband, but not all Rooks are flat enough at the top to stand up (also, no Rook may be available).

223. Whatever kind of piece a Pawn is promoted to is the kind it must be for the remainder of the game. Once a Pawn is promoted to a Knight, it is always a Knight.

224. Promoted pieces are just as vulnerable to capture as natural ones. Promoted pieces have no additional powers.

225. To summarize, a Pawn cannot—

(a) promote to a King,
(b) remain as a Pawn after promotion,
(c) change to another chessman after it has been promoted to a particular one.

EN PASSANT

226. If you have trouble with this section, skip it for now. It is not immediately relevant to what follows and can be reconsidered later.

227. The least understood and most questioned rule of chess is the rule of *en passant*. (Many people play chess without even knowing this rule.) It refers to a certain kind of Pawn capture.

228. *En passant* is a French expression that means *in passing*. If a Pawn tries to pass an opposing Pawn by moving two squares, it can be captured in passing.

229. You can capture by *en passant* or be captured by *en passant*.

230. We see how this works in the next three diagrams. In diagram 100 it is Black's move.

DIAGRAM 100

Black's turn to play

231. Suppose Black moves his King Pawn two squares, from his K2 to his K4 (trying to avoid being captured).

DIAGRAM 101

after Black's move

232. White may pretend Black's Pawn had moved only one square and may capture it as if it had advanced only one square. Diagram 102 shows the position after White captures Black's King Pawn by *en passant.*

DIAGRAM 102

after White's move

233. You do not have to capture a Pawn by *en passant* simply because you can. You may ignore the possibility of capture and play another move instead. But if you want to capture by *en passant,* you must capture on your next move.

234. If you delay the capture of an enemy Pawn by *en passant* for even 1 move, you lose the right to capture that particular Pawn in the *en passant* way.

235. During the course of a game (and if the situation arises)—

   (a) any Pawn may capture or be captured by *en passant,*
   (b) both White and Black may capture by *en passant* as many times as desired.

236. For *en passant* to be possible—

    (a)   both the captured and capturing Pawns must be on adjacent files,

    (b)   the Pawn to be captured must have just exercised its two-square, first-move option (trying to avoid capture).

237. Diagrams 103–105 illustrate *en passant* capturing for Black.

DIAGRAMS 103–105
En passant *Capturing for Black*

White to play

Black to play

after capturing by *en passant*

238. *Question:* According to diagrams 106 and 107, can White capture Black's Pawn by *en passant*?

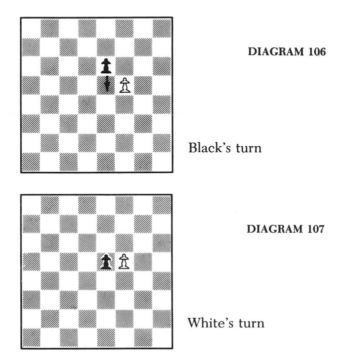

DIAGRAM 106

Black's turn

DIAGRAM 107

White's turn

239. *Answer:* No, because Black did not exercise his two-square, first-move option. Black's move was actually the second time the Black Pawn had moved in the game.

THE EXCHANGE VALUES OF THE PIECES

240. The object of chess is to checkmate the opposing King, but this is not always so easy. Usually before

you can force checkmate you must have some concrete, clear advantage.

241. Many different kinds of factors determine who has the ultimate advantage in a chess position. The easiest factor to weigh is the strength of the armies. If you have the stronger army, you will usually be able to force checkmate, given enough time.

242. Advantages in material are not only determined by the number of chessmen, but also by the kind. Generally, a chessman's relative value is based on the number of squares it can move to, guard, and influence.

243. The term *mobility* refers to the number of different squares a chessman can move to in any given position. The more squares a piece can move to, the greater its mobility.

244. *Space* and mobility are related terms. If a chessman has greater mobility than another, it controls more space than another.

245. Since captures are common in a chess game, it is important to have a way to evaluate each one. In capturing, try to get at least as much as you give up.

246. Before examining the relative values of the chess-men, remember that—

    (a) you win material when you get more than you give up,

    (b) you lose material when you get less than you give up,

    (c) you trade material when you get the same as you give up.

247. Some beginners mistakenly say "lose" when they really mean "trade." Consequently, they think to trade the Queen means to lose it. There's a big difference.

248. Since Pawns are the weakest chessmen, they are used as the basic unit of chess value. Pawns have an exchange value of 1.

249. The next valuable chessman is the Knight. It is worth about 3 Pawns.

250. Bishops are about equal to Knights, but both pieces obviously have different powers. A Bishop is also worth about 3 Pawns.

251. A Rook is worth about 5 Pawns, which is equal to a Knight and 2 Pawns, or a Bishop and 2 Pawns.

252. A Queen, because it combines the powers of both Rook and Bishop, is worth slightly more than the sum

of both pieces. A Queen is worth about 9 Pawns, which is about equal to a Rook, Bishop, and Pawn, which is about equal to a Rook, Knight, and Pawn.

253. The King does not have an exchange value, for it can never be given up.

254. These relative values stem from the experience of good players through the centuries. The word *relative* not only implies that each value is based on the value of other chessmen, but also that each value depends on the position at hand.

255. For example, if a piece is placed badly, its value is reduced. If a piece is placed well, its value is increased.

256. Generally, a Pawn on its seventh rank about to Queen is more valuable than a Pawn on its third rank under attack.

257. An attacking Bishop may be more valuable than a defending Rook, while a centralized Knight may be more deadly than a misplaced Queen.

258. The key point to remember is that these values are not absolute: Time, circumstance, and other relations influence them. In the overwelming majority of positions, however, these values can be trusted.

CHART OF THE RELATIVE EXCHANGE VALUES OF THE CHESSMEN

CHESSMAN	EQUALS
Pawn	1 Pawn
Knight	3 Pawns
Bishop	3 Pawns
Rook	5 Pawns
Queen	9 Pawns
King	no exchange value

HOW TO RECORD A GAME

259. It is possible to keep a written record of the moves of a chess game. Writing the moves down is called *keeping score*. (You can read a chess game as you can a musical composition.)

260. In keeping score, moves are not written out, but abbreviated by way of a notational system.

261. There are two different notational systems commonly used in English-speaking countries: the descriptive system and the algebraic system.

262. This book uses the *descriptive system* because it appears more often in American and English publications.

263. There are four reasons chess games are recorded:

    (a) To settle disputes (especially in tournament play)
    (b) For chess history (every subject is enchanced by a sense of its own history)
    (c) For personal reasons (how well did you play ten years ago?)
    (d) To read chess books (so that you can learn how to play)

264. Usually, four bits of information are recorded in the descriptive system:

    (a) The number of the move
    (b) Which chessman moves
    (c) What the chessman does
    (d) Where it goes

265. The descriptive system is so named because it describes the movement of the chessmen in terms of their names. It utilizes the same names for the pieces and parts of the board already given in this book. The following chart gives some of those names and their respective abbreviations.

NAME	ABBREVIATION
Queen Rook	QR
Queen Knight	QN
Queen Bishop	QB
Queen	Q
King	K
King Bishop	KB
King Knight	KN
King Rook	KR
Queen Rook Pawn	QRP
Queen Knight Pawn	QNP
Queen Bishop Pawn	QBP
Queen Pawn	QP
King Pawn	KP
King Bishop Pawn	KBP
King Knight Pawn	KNP
King Rook Pawn	KRP

266. Here are some other abbreviations you must know before you can record a game.

SYMBOL	MEANING
–	moves to
x	captures
O–O	castles Kingside
O–O–O	castles Queenside
ch	check
e.p.	*en passant*
!	good move
!!	very good move

SYMBOL	MEANING
?	bad move
??	very bad move
(R/Q3)	Rook on Queen 3 (in case we want to refer to a piece and the square it's on)

267. Earlier we looked at the fool's mate (Number 137). Let's see how that 2-move game is recorded. Remember to give the White name for a particular square when White moves to that square and give the Black name for a particular square when Black moves to that square.

THE FOOL'S MATE

268. White's first move:

DIAGRAM 108

1 **P–KB3** (Pawn to King Bishop 3)

(*1*)	= the move number
(**P**)	= the chessman that moves
(**–**)	= what the chessman does
(**KB3**)	= the square it moves to

269. Black's first move:

DIAGRAM 109

1 . . . **P–K4** (Pawn to King 4)

270. White's second move:

DIAGRAM 110

2 **P–KN4** (Pawn to King Knight 4)

271. Black's second move:

DIAGRAM 111

2 . . . **Q–R5 mate** (Queen to Rook 5 mate)

272. Notice that in the above recording, three periods precede the Black moves to distinguish them from the White ones. (This is done when the Black moves are presented independently of White moves.)

273. On a score sheet, the fool's mate would look like this:

WHITE	BLACK
1 **P–KB3**	**P–K4**
2 **P–KN4**	**Q–R5 mate**

274. If you wish to record your own games and haven't got any score sheets, make your own from the model.

275. You have now completed the first part of your course. You know how to play chess, but you still

don't know how to play well. The second half of the book discusses the right things to do. It is slightly harder, and some of its statements may be confusing at first.

276. Try as best you can to understand the more difficult parts of the book. If you cannot understand the point of a particular statement, read on. You can always reread the confusing statement after you've had more experience. You don't have to understand every small point to improve your game or to read this book.

	QR8	QN8	QB8	Q8	K8	KB8	KN8	KR8	
8	QR1	QN1	QB1	Q1	K1	KB1	KN1	KR1	1
7	QR7	QN7	QB7	Q7	K7	KB7	KN7	KR7	2
	QR2	QN2	QB2	Q2	K2	KB2	KN2	KR2	
6	QR6	QN6	QB6	Q6	K6	KB6	KN6	KR6	3
	QR3	QN3	QB3	Q3	K3	KB3	KN3	KR3	
5	QR5	QN5	QB5	Q5	K5	KB5	KN5	KR5	4
	QR4	QN4	QB4	Q4	K4	KB4	KN4	KR4	
4	QR4	QN4	QB4	Q4	K4	KB4	KN4	KR4	5
	QR5	QN5	QB5	Q5	K5	KB5	KN5	KR5	
3	QR3	QN3	QB3	Q3	K3	KB3	KN3	KR3	6
	QR6	QN6	QB6	Q6	K6	KB6	KN6	KR6	
2	QR2	QN2	QB2	Q2	K2	KB2	KN2	KR2	7
	QR7	QN7	QB7	Q7	K7	KB7	KN7	KR7	
1	QR1	QN1	QB1	Q1	K1	KB1	KN1	KR1	8
	QR8	QN8	QB8	Q8	K8	KB8	KN8	KR8	

White

CHAPTER 4

Winning Material

277. Unless your opponent plays badly, it is not possible to mate him early in the game. Even if he does play badly, he can probably avoid mate for many moves. You won't be able to look that far ahead and picture the actual mating position in your mind.

278. From a practical point of view, you should not play for mate at the start. Instead, you should play for smaller, more immediate gains.

279. You should try to get the advantage. Whoever has the better position has the advantage. Usually, if you have the advantage you can force mate eventually.

280. Various factors determine who has the overall advantage in a chess position.

281. The easiest factor to understand and evaluate is material.

282. Advantages in material are based on the strength of your army versus the strength of your opponent's.

283. If all other things are equal, the stronger army wins. If you win material you should be able to force mate.

284. The main way to win material is by a double attack.

285. A *double attack* is an aggressive move that threatens the enemy in at least two different ways.

286. Double attacks are examples of tactics.

287. Two words that are often confused are *strategy* and *tactics*.

288. Strategy is the overall plan and is long term; tactics are the individual operations to bring about that plan and are short term.

289. Strategy is what you are going to do; tactics are how you are going to do it. Always keep in mind the distinction between the two words.

290. Tactics are as much as 95 percent of a chess game. If you know tactics, you really know chess.

291. It is time to examine the two most important double attack tactics:

(a) the fork
(b) the pin

292. The *fork* is a tactic by which one chessman directly· attacks two or more enemy chessmen on the same move.

293. Every chessman can fork.

294. Diagram 112 illustrates a Knight fork. The White Knight is attacking the Black King and the Black Queen at the same time.

DIAGRAM 112
A Knight Fork

295.   After Black moves his King out of check the White Knight will be able to capture the Black Queen.

296.   Diagram 113 shows a Pawn fork. The White Pawn attacks the Black Knight and the Black Rook.

DIAGRAM 113
A Pawn Fork

297.   Black must lose either his Knight or his Rook. If Black moves the Rook away, the White Pawn can take the Black Knight; if Black moves the Knight away, the White Pawn can take the Black Rook.

298.   Diagram 114 shows a Bishop fork. The White Bishop attacks the Black King, the Black Rook, and the Black Knight.

DIAGRAM 114
A Bishop Fork

299.   After Black moves his King out of check, the White Bishop will be able to capture either the Black Rook or the Black Knight.

300.   Diagram 115 shows a Rook fork. The White Rook attacks the Black King, the Black Bishop, the Black Knight, and the Black Pawn.

DIAGRAM 115
A Rook Fork

301.   Diagram 116 shows a Queen fork. The White Queen attacks the Black King, the Black Rook, the Black Knight, the Black Bishop, and four Black Pawns.

DIAGRAM 116
A Queen Fork

302. White to play can fork Black in diagram 117. Find White's forking move.

DIAGRAM 117

303. The solution is *1 N–B7ch.* (This is read: Knight to Bishop 7 check.) After Black gets his King out of check, the White Knight can capture the Black Rook.

DIAGRAM 118

DIAGRAM 119

304. In diagram 120 White can win the Black Rook in 2
moves. Find the fork.

DIAGRAM 120

305. The solution is *1 QxPch*, (this is read: Queen takes
Pawn check), forking the Black King and the Black
Rook.

DIAGRAM 121

306. Black will then have to get his King to safety. For
example, he could play *1 . . . K–N2*. (This is read:
King to Knight 2.)

DIAGRAM 122

307. Then White can capture the Black Rook: *2* **QxR.** (This is read: Queen takes Rook.)

DIAGRAM 123

308. Forks are easy to understand, whereas pins are harder to grasp. The *pin* is a tactic that prevents an enemy piece from moving off a rank, file, or diagonal because to do so would expose another piece or an important square to attack.

309. Pins usually involve at least one attacker and two enemy chessmen (*targets*).

310. The attacker and its two enemy targets must all be on the same rank, file, or diagonal. In other words a straight line can be drawn through all three chessmen.

311. Diagram 124 shows a simple pin and should help you to understand the concept.

DIAGRAM 124
A Simple Pin

312. The White Rook attacks the Black Knight. Black would like to move his Knight out of attack but can't, for that would expose his King to attack. Thus, the Black Knight is frozen, or pinned.

313. A pinned piece cannot move off the line of the pin.

314. In diagram 124 the White Rook is the pinner.

315. It is said that the White Rook pins the Black Knight to the Black King.

316. Notice that all three chessmen, the pinner and the two targets, lie along a straight line.

317. If you want to use your imagination, picture the Rook as the head of a straight pin, the Knight as a sheet of paper, and the King as a bulletin board.

318. This resemblance to a real metal pin explains the origin of the word.

319. Only Bishops, Rooks, and Queens can pin.

320. There are two kinds of pins:
    (a) Absolute pins
    (b) Relative pins

321. An *absolute pin* is a pin to the King—the pinned chessman cannot move away.

322. A *relative pin* is a pin to any other chessman. The pinned chessman can move away, but it is usually undesirable to do so.

323. Diagram 124 shows an absolute pin. It is illegal for Black to move his Knight away.

324. Diagram 125 shows a relative pin.

325. In diagram 125 the White Bishop pins the Black Rook to the Black Queen. The Black Rook could move away, but that would enable the White Bishop to take the Black Queen. In some circumstances, you may allow your Queen to be taken, but here it is undesirable.

326. In diagram 125, even if it's Black's turn to move, White is going to win at least a Rook for a Bishop. Since the Black Rook must stay where it is to shield the Black Queen, the White Bishop will be able to capture the Black Rook on the next move.

327. Diagrams 126–132 show an important pinning sequence.

DIAGRAM 126

328. White to play can pin the Black Bishop to the Black King by **R–K1.**

DIAGRAM 127

329. Black cannot save the Bishop by moving it away because it's pinned to his King. Still, Black can at least protect the Bishop by *1 . . .* **P–Q4.**

DIAGRAM 128

330. White won't take the Black Bishop with his Rook because that entails losing a Rook (worth 5) in return for gaining a Bishop (worth 3).

331. But there is no need to take the Bishop yet; it can't run away. The pinned chessman is stuck and help-less.

332. If a pinned chessman is protected, try to attack it again—especially with a Pawn.

333. In diagram 129 White attacks the Black Bishop again with a Pawn: 2 **P–Q3.**

DIAGRAM 129

334. Now the Bishop is lost for sure. Even if Black protects it again, White will only have to give up a Pawn to capture it. For example, Black could protect the Bishop by *2 . . .* **P–B4**.

DIAGRAM 130

335. The Black Bishop is protected twice, but White takes it anyway by *3* **PxB**.

DIAGRAM 131

336. Though it's true that Black can win a Pawn for his Bishop, he still has lost material. Play might continue: *3 . . .* **QPxP**.

DIAGRAM 132

337. The damage has been done. Black has lost a Bishop for a Pawn—all because the Bishop was pinned.

338. Try to pin your opponent's pieces. Avoid putting your own chessmen in pins.

339. Don't always capture pinned pieces right away. In some cases it is better to attack them again, preferably with a Pawn. Remember: Pinned pieces are helpless and can't move away.

340. Some pins can be broken. There are three ways to break pins:

    (a) Moving the pinned piece away and accepting the consequences (this can only happen if the pin is a relative one)
    (b) Blocking the line between the pinner and the pinned chessman
    (c) Moving the back target away with a counter-threat

341. Diagram 133 shows a relative pin that can be safely broken.

DIAGRAM 133

342. Although the Black Rook is pinned to his Queen by the White Bishop, Black can move his Rook and break the pin by *1 . . .* **R–B8ch.**

DIAGRAM 134

343. Now the White Bishop is unable to capture the Black Queen, since White must first respond to the check.

The check gives the Queen time to move away. White must play *2* **K–N2,** getting out of check.

DIAGRAM 135

344. Now Black can safely move his Queen away.

345. If there was a White Rook on KB1 in diagram 133, then Black would not be able to break the pin with a Rook check.

DIAGRAM 136

346. Here the move *1 . . .* **R–B8** would not be a check, and so if Black played *1 . . .* **R–B8** , then White could continue with **BxQ**, winning the Queen.

DIAGRAM 137   **DIAGRAM 138**

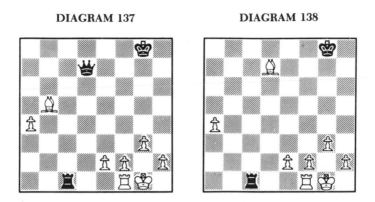

347. Another way to break a pin is to stick something in the way.

DIAGRAM 139

348. Here the Black Queen is pinned to her King by the White Rook. But Black can break the pin and save his

Queen by putting his own Rook in the way: *1 . . .*
R–K4.

DIAGRAM 140

349. Finally, it is sometimes possible to break a pin by
     moving the back target away and making a strong
     counterthreat.

DIAGRAM 141

350. In diagram 141 the Black Rook is pinned to his
     Queen by the White Bishop. Black can break the pin,
     however, by *1 . . .* **Q–N2ch.**

DIAGRAM 142

351. After White gets out of check, Black will be able to move his Rook safely away.

352. There are other important tactics, but pins and forks are the most significant because they come up in almost every game.

353. The sections on mating patterns and winning material both demonstrate the powers of the pieces and Pawns. There are other factors in chess besides mate and material, and we shall come to them shortly. For now, look for double attacks—pins and forks.

Black

8	QR1 / QR8	QN1 / QN8	QB1 / QB8	Q1 / Q8	K1 / K8	KB1 / KB8	KN1 / KN8	KR1 / KR8	**1**
7	QR2 / QR7	QN2 / QN7	QB2 / QB7	Q2 / Q7	K2 / K7	KB2 / KB7	KN2 / KN7	KR2 / KR7	**2**
6	QR3 / QR6	QN3 / QN6	QB3 / QB6	Q3 / Q6	K3 / K6	KB3 / KB6	KN3 / KN6	KR3 / KR6	**3**
5	QR4 / QR5	QN4 / QN5	QB4 / QB5	Q4 / Q5	K4 / K5	KB4 / KB5	KN4 / KN5	KR4 / KR5	**4**
4	QR5 / QR4	QN5 / QN4	QB5 / QB4	Q5 / Q4	K5 / K4	KB5 / KB4	KN5 / KN4	KR5 / KR4	**5**
3	QR6 / QR3	QN6 / QN3	QB6 / QB3	Q6 / Q3	K6 / K3	KB6 / KB3	KN6 / KN3	KR6 / KR3	**6**
2	QR7 / QR2	QN7 / QN2	QB7 / QB2	Q7 / Q2	K7 / K2	KB7 / KB2	KN7 / KN2	KR7 / KR2	**7**
1	QR8 / QR1	QN8 / QN1	QB8 / QB1	Q8 / Q1	K8 / K1	KB8 / KB1	KN8 / KN1	KR8 / KR1	**8**

White

CHAPTER 5

Principles

354. *Principles* are general statements that suggest things to do or not to do. They should be followed, unless there is a definite reason for violating them.

355. *Rules* are regulations and restrictions that must be obeyed.

356. In chess, first you learn the rules (how to play) and then you learn the principles (how to play well).

357. The difference between rules and principles can be illustrated with regard to castling. The rule is that you move the King two squares toward the Rook and then bring the Rook to the other side of the King. The principle is that you should castle early in the game.

358. The rule is always true; the principle is usually true.

359. A single principle can apply to millions of chess positions.

360. To apply a principle you simply have to know what kind of position you're examining. You don't have to understand all the possibilities.

361. Principles are helpful when you are confused. You might ask, "What does the principle suggest I do in this kind of position?"

362. It is much easier to find a kind of move than a specific move. It is far easier to learn twenty general ideas than to memorize millions of particular chess positions.

363. If you play by the principles you may not find the best move, but you should be able to find a reasonable one.

364. From here on, the most important principles will be discussed in depth. Learn them, use them, master them; but don't become discouraged if you have difficulty.

365. When a particular principle or practical statement confuses you, accept it temporarily. You may come to understand it when you find that it works.

THE OPENING

366. The opening is the beginning part of a chess game. It usually lasts 10 to 15 moves.

367. There is no best opening move, but for beginners playing White, I recommend moving the King Pawn two squares.

368. Since White moves first, he starts with a slight advantage.

369. In most positions, it is better to attack than to defend. In battle the first strike is often decisive.

370. The attacker has a practical advantage: If he makes a mistake, sometimes he can recover. But if the defender makes a mistake, he loses.

371. Because the attacker forces the play, he has the *initiative*.

372.   You have the initiative if you can control and direct the course of events—if you can force the action. The attacker has the initiative; the defender tries to take it. The attacker directs the action; the defender responds to it. In theory (but not in practice), the attacker is trying to win and the defender is trying to draw.

373.   Since White starts as the attacker, he has the winning chances. (In tournament play he wins about 60 percent of the time.)

374.   Some good players disregard theory and try to win with both White and Black. With Black they blend defense and counterattack, leading to sharp, tense, complicated play. To win they are willing to risk defeat.

375.   Though it is more fun to attack, don't attack blindly. Pay attention to your opponent's moves.

376.   Don't memorize and play the same set of opening moves, regardless of enemy responses. Reason is clearly superior to memory.

377.   The opening is dependent on the interaction between you and your opponent. Neither side plans its moves in a vacuum. Each must respond to enemy play.

378.   Although there is no best opening move, there is a best opening plan—*play for the center.*

379. To play for the center means to occupy, guard, and influence the squares in the very center of the board: K4, K5, Q4, and Q5 (from now on called *the center*).

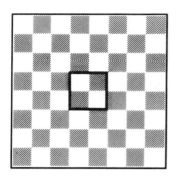

DIAGRAM 143
The Center

380. The squares that surround the center are also important.

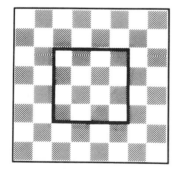

DIAGRAM 144
The Enlarged Center

381. From the start, both sides should actively fight for the center. While there are various ways to do this, the simplest is to occupy the center.

382. You should try to occupy the center for at least three reasons:

    (a)   To prepare for action
    (b)   To restrict the enemy
    (c)   To increase mobility

383. To prepare for action: Pieces in the center can move to either side of the board more quickly and easily than they can from anywhere else. You are more prepared for sudden changes when your pieces occupy the center.

384. To restrict the enemy: Pieces in the center keep the enemy from organizing his forces. They present a barrier.

385. To increase mobility: Pieces in the center have greater mobility. They can move to more squares.

386. Every piece except the Rook has greater mobility in the center than the corner. The Knight needs the center the most and the Rook needs the center the least.

387. Central occupation, however, doesn't guarantee central control. Since no chessman guards itself, the square it occupies is not necessarily secure.

388. Ideally, try both to occupy and to protect the center.

389. There are other ways to influence the center, but you must be more experienced to appreciate them. For now, simply occupy and guard.

DEVELOPMENT

390. Victory in chess usually depends on who gets there first with the most.

391. In the opening, you should mobilize all your forces as soon as you can. This is the principle of *development.*

392. To develop a piece is to increase its potential by moving it from its original square to a useful one, or by moving another chessman out of its way.

393. The two great opening principles, centralization and development, actually combine into a more comprehensive one: Develop your pieces toward the center.

394. Try to develop a new piece on each move.

395. Try to move each piece once before moving any piece twice. (Don't confuse Pawns and pieces. A Pawn is not a piece.)

396. But don't develop mechanically. Develop each piece to the best available square.

397. Try to make Pawn moves that contribute to development. Pawn moves should open lines for new pieces to come out.

398. In the opening, the two best Pawns for a beginner to move are the Queen and King Pawns (the two center Pawns).

399. Don't move other Pawns unless clearly necessary or desirable. If you're not sure about the strength of a Pawn move, don't make it.

400. Try to move the center Pawns two squares each, to form a *classical Pawn center.*

DIAGRAM 145
The Classical Pawn Center

401. In diagram 145 the White Pawns occupy two central squares (Q4 and K4) and guard the other ones (Q5 and K5). In addition, the Queen Pawn is already protected by the Queen.

402. Moreover, White is able to develop all his pieces without moving another Pawn.

403. If Black doesn't interfere, White can develop all his pieces in 8 more moves from the position given in diagram 145.

404. A sample variation of 8 moves is presented in diagrams 146–153. Each move is given in chess notation alongside its respective diagram.

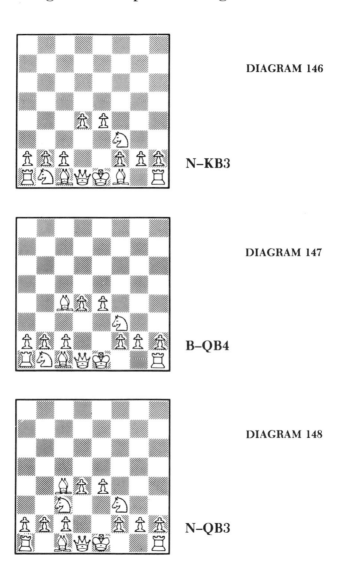

DIAGRAM 146

N–KB3

DIAGRAM 147

B–QB4

DIAGRAM 148

N–QB3

DIAGRAM 149

B–KB4

DIAGRAM 150

0–0 (castles)

DIAGRAM 151

Q–Q3

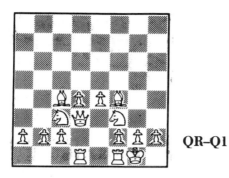

DIAGRAM 152

QR–Q1

DIAGRAM 153

KR–K1

405. Usually development is completed by moving all the pieces and by castling.

406. The order of development is important. Develop the minor pieces first (Knights and Bishops).

407. The principle is: Knights before Bishops.

408. Knights should be developed first, mainly because they need more time to reach the enemy. To be effective they must be up close, so they need a head start.

409. Each Knight basically has only one good developing move, regardless of what the enemy does. Knights should be developed to the enlarged center.

410. Most of the time, both the White Knight and Black Knight on KN1 should move to their KB3. Both the White Knight and Black Knight on QN1 should move to their QB3. A Knight on KB3 or QB3 controls eight squares. On its starting square, the Knight controls only three squares.

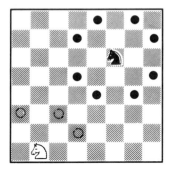

DIAGRAM 154

411. Unlike the Knight, the Bishop may have a few good developing moves, depending on what the enemy does. Bishops should be developed to open diagonals (diagonals not blocked by Pawns).

412. Since early in a game you are more sure of where to move the Knights than where to move the Bishops, you should move at least one of your Knights before moving any of your Bishops (unless you have a very good reason for moving a Bishop first). Moving a Knight first is less risky and less committal.

413. Actually, since Kingside castling is often safer than Queenside castling (because castling Kingside gets the King out of the exposed center one move sooner), there is a more specific developing order to consider.

414. You should consider developing the Kingside minor pieces before developing the Queenside ones, so that castling Kingside is possible right away.

415. To be specific, develop the Kingside Knight, then the Kingside Bishop, then the Queenside Knight, and then the Queenside Bishop. (Remember: The Queenside is made up of the QR, QN, QB, and Q files while the Kingside is made up of the K, KB, KN, and KR files.

416. Castling is usually a developing move because it enables a Rook to come to the center. Castling gets the King out of the way and enables the Rooks to protect each other.

417. But castling can be a defensive move too. It gets the King out of the exposed center. (An area is usually more exposed if its Pawns have moved.)

418. Castling puts the King behind a wall of Pawns (if you haven't moved the Pawns on the castling side).

419. After castling, don't move the Pawns in front of your King unless you must. Try to keep a wall of protection between yourself and the enemy forces. The word *castling* and the move it indicates come from the idea of medieval noblemen fortifying themselves in real castles.

420. The principle is: Castle early.

421. Rooks should be developed to *open files* (files unoccupied by Pawns), *half-open files* (files occupied just by enemy Pawns), or files that are likely to open (files with advanced friendly Pawns that may soon be exchanged for enemy Pawns).

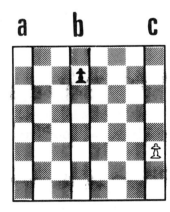

DIAGRAM 155

(a) An open file
(b) A half-open file for White
(c) A half-open file for Black

422. The principle is: Rooks belong on open files.

423. The point is that on open files Rooks can attack and penetrate the enemy position easily, whereas on closed files Rooks cannot attack the enemy at all because a friendly Pawn gets in the way.

424. A related principle is: Rooks belong on half-open files. The point is that on half-open files Rooks can attack enemy Pawns.

425. In diagram 156, the White Rooks should move to the half-open QN and K files while the Black Rooks should move to the half-open Q and QR files.

DIAGRAM 156

426. Try to control *open lines* (the files, ranks, and diagonals that have no Pawns in the way).

427. Rooks need open files and ranks. Bishops need open diagonals. The Queen needs open files, ranks, and diagonals.

428. The Queen, the Rooks, and the Bishops are long-range pieces. They work effectively from a distance if there are no Pawns in the way.

429. Lines blocked by Pawns are *closed*, for usually Pawns cannot be moved out of the way easily. Lines blocked by pieces are *semi-open*, for pieces probably can be moved out of the way easily.

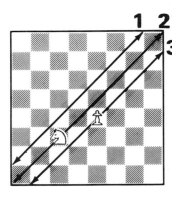

DIAGRAM 157

Diagonal 1 is open
Diagonal 2 is semi-open
Diagonal 3 is closed

430. If you control the open lines you control the gateways to the enemy position.

431. In the opening, try to develop with threats.

432. For the most part, a *threat* is a direct attack. You can threaten to capture an enemy chessman or to checkmate the enemy King.

433. Threats force responses. You couldn't ignore a threat to your person. You shouldn't ignore a threat to your game.

434. You gain time when you develop with a threat.

435. To *gain time* is to force an opponent's response or to complete an action in fewer moves than it normally takes.

436. If you gain time you gain moves. If you lose time you lose moves.

437. Don't bring out the Queen early. You may be tempted to forget this principle. You might think only of the Queen's power and not of the possibility of losing it.

438. A Queen developed too early is subject to attack. A lone Queen can't do much anyway. It needs support. As in a play, the supporting cast should be introduced first.

439. In diagram 158 the Black Queen is exposed.

DIAGRAM 158

440. In diagram 159 White can play **N–QB3**, developing a Knight and threatening the Black Queen.

DIAGRAM 159

441. Black could still try to keep his Queen in the center with **Q–Q5**.

DIAGRAM 160

442. But that enables White to develop the other Knight with a threat to the Black Queen. White should play **N–B3** (gaining time on the Black Queen).

DIAGRAM 161

443. Notice that together the White Knights guard the four central squares.

444. Suppose in diagram 161 Black moves **Q–B4**.

DIAGRAM 162

445. White could then open the diagonal of his Queenside Bishop and threaten the Black Queen by **P–Q4**. (The Pawn is protected by both the White Queen on Q1 and the White Knight on KB3).

DIAGRAM 163

446. Suppose Black responds by moving his Queen to QB3.

DIAGRAM 164

447. White could then develop a new piece and pin the Black Queen: **B–QN5**.

DIAGRAM 165

448. The White Bishop pins the Black Queen to the Black King. If Black tries to defend by taking the White Bishop with his Queen . . .

DIAGRAM 166

449. . . . then White captures the Black Queen with his Knight.

DIAGRAM 167

450. White was able to make 4 developing moves at Black's expense (3 piece moves and 1 Pawn move that opened lines). It can't be said enough: Don't bring the Queen out early.

451. If your opponent brings his Queen out early, try to attack it and develop at the same time. Take advantage of his time-wasting moves.

452. But don't just attack the enemy Queen haphazardly; try to build, improve, and develop your position at the same time.

453. You may be tempted to violate the principles simply because you are playing another beginner. You may think that other beginners are too weak to take advantage of risky play. Good players never take such chances—that's why they're good.

454. Think about it. If your opponent is truly weak he is just as likely to play a good move as a bad one. His response is totally random.

455. At this point, even though you may have many questions, the importance of centralization and development should be obvious.

It is time to move on.

	8	7	6	5	4	3	2	1	
8	QR1 / QR8	QN1 / QN8	QB1 / QB8	Q1 / Q8	K1 / K8	KB1 / KB8	KN1 / KN8	KR1 / KR8	**1**
7	QR2 / QR7	QN2 / QN7	QB2 / QB7	Q2 / Q7	K2 / K7	KB2 / KB7	KN2 / KN7	KR2 / KR7	**2**
6	QR3 / QR6	QN3 / QN6	QB3 / QB6	Q3 / Q6	K3 / K6	KB3 / KB6	KN3 / KN6	KR3 / KR6	**3**
5	QR4 / QR5	QN4 / QN5	QB4 / QB5	Q4 / Q5	K4 / K5	KB4 / KB5	KN4 / KN5	KR4 / KR5	**4**
4	QR5 / QR4	QN5 / QN4	QB5 / QB4	Q5 / Q4	K5 / K4	KB5 / KB4	KN5 / KN4	KR5 / KR4	**5**
3	QR6 / QR3	QN6 / QN3	QB6 / QB3	Q6 / Q3	K6 / K3	KB6 / KB3	KN6 / KN3	KR6 / KR3	**6**
2	QR7 / QR2	QN7 / QN2	QB7 / QB2	Q7 / Q2	K7 / K2	KB7 / KB2	KN7 / KN2	KR7 / KR2	**7**
1	QR8 / QR1	QN8 / QN1	QB8 / QB1	Q8 / Q1	K8 / K1	KB8 / KB1	KN8 / KN1	KR8 / KR1	**8**

White

CHAPTER 6

Chess Thinking

456. In the study of any subject, problems may arise that can't be answered immediately.

457. Especially in chess, some situations and concepts require considerable experience before they can be understood.

458. Be practical. You don't have to understand every detail to play chess well. Remember that if a statement confuses you, accept it as being true and go on. After a while, the ideas should fall into place.

459. There are many facets to chess study. More important than memorizing specific facts is knowing how to examine a chess position.

460. A critical evaluation of a chess position is called an *analysis*.

461. To analyze a chess position is to break it down into its key elements—to determine who stands better.

462. Among the numerous factors considered in an analysis are material, mobility, development, Pawn structure, and King safety.

463. There are five basic conclusions:

(a) White stands better (White has more winning chances than Black)
(b) Black stands better (Black has more winning chances than White)
(c) The game is even (both sides have equal chances of winning)
(d) White is winning
(e) Black is winning

464. Good players seldom look more than a few moves ahead. Anyway, to look far ahead is unnecessary and impractical.

465. Good players play by the principles and place great faith in the laws of probability.

466. In chess, 99 percent of the unforeseen possibilities can be dealt with as they arise. Therefore, it wastes time and energy to look deeply into most positions.

467. The laws of chess ensure that if you have a winning position, regardless of what the enemy does, you can ultimately convert the winning position into mate. You may still have to find some very good moves along the way, but at least you know the moves are there to be found (and that's a great help).

468. Although I can't prove to you that the laws of chess work, centuries of chess history confirm that they do. For now you must simply accept that they do until you've had more experience—until you've lost many games. Actually, since every game you lose is a learning experience, the more games you lose the better player you will eventually be.

469. Once you accept that a winning position should lead to mate, you need to know what a winning position looks like and what kinds of advantages lead to mate.

470. Though some winning advantages are not obvious, others are easy to see.

471. Most material advantages are clear and understandable. However, at first you may have trouble capitalizing on all but the most overwhelming ones.

472. Masters usually can win with as little as an extra Pawn, but at first you may not be able to win with an extra Queen.

473. Nonmaterial factors can be equally important but are harder to take advantage of. You should be able to sense that a powerful attack against a defenseless King, a great lead in development, and a vast superiority in space are obvious factors. You probably just don't have the technique to win consistently with these advantages.

474. *Technique* is the way you perform a certain task.

475. You can have better technique and more technique. Everyone has technique, but no two players have the same technique. Since technique is primarily determined by experience, veterans must have better and more technique than you do. Thus the best way to acquire technique is to play.

476. Good players never stop learning. They constantly observe the play of others. They read chess books and try to solve problems (sometimes the same ones over and over). And after losing, they eagerly examine the game with their opponent.

477. Remember: At every stage you will encounter problems that are beyond you. Try your best to solve them, but if you still don't understand, play and read on. All you need is more experience.

Fortunately, chess can be enjoyed at all levels, and there are very few activities for which that is true.

Black

8	QR8	QN8	QB8	Q8	K8	KB8	KN8	KR8	**1**
7	QR7	QN7	QB7	Q7	K7	KB7	KN7	KR7	**2**
6	QR6	QN6	QB6	Q6	K6	KB6	KN6	KR6	**3**
5	QR5	QN5	QB5	Q5	K5	KB5	KN5	KR5	**4**
4	QR4	QN4	QB4	Q4	K4	KB4	KN4	KR4	**5**
3	QR3	QN3	QB3	Q3	K3	KB3	KN3	KR3	**6**
2	QR2	QN2	QB2	Q2	K2	KB2	KN2	KR2	**7**
1	QR1	QN1	QB1	Q1	K1	KB1	KN1	KR1	**8**

White

CHAPTER 7

AN ACTUAL GAME

478. It is now time to consider a real chess game. In our particular example, the White moves are played by a chess master and the Black by a beginner. Try to follow the moves, alternatives, and explanations as closely as you can, but don't get bogged down in small points. Since you must have an overall picture

before you can understand some particular points, play through the entire game even if you become confused.

479. White begins with *1* **P–K4**.

DIAGRAM 168

480. In your own games you should also make this opening move because it leads to positions that are easier to understand. The Pawn guards a central square (Q5) and opens the way for White's Queen and Bishop.

Bobby Fischer, the famous American chess player, once jokingly said that the move *1* **P–K4** was "best by test."

481. For similar reasons, Black responds *1* . . . **P–K4**.

DIAGRAM 169

482. Now both sides have a share of the center and can develop the same pieces, but White still has the initiative.

483. White continues *2* **N–KB3**, developing a new piece and threatening the Black King Pawn.

DIAGRAM 170

484. The best way for Black to protect the King Pawn is 2 . . . N–QB3, for it also develops a piece toward the center.

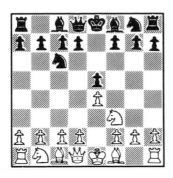

DIAGRAM 171

485. But Black doesn't play 2 . . . N–QB3. (Don't confuse what could have happened with what did.)

486. Another reasonable response would have been 2 . . . P–Q3, solidly protecting the King Pawn and opening the diagonal of the light square Bishop.

DIAGRAM 172

487. But Black doesn't play that either. Instead he plays the questionable 2 . . . **P–KB3?** (A question mark after a move means the move is a mistake.)

DIAGRAM 173

488. This move is bad because—

    (a) it doesn't contribute to development (no new piece can come out),

    (b) it blocks KB3, depriving the Black King Knight of its best square,

    (c) it weakens the position of the Black King (it will now be possible to attack the Black King along its K1–KR4 diagonal),

    (d) it enables White to prevent Black from castling Kingside (White can post his Bishop on QB4 and guard KN8).

489. White now considers a piece sacrifice, trying to take advantage of the weakened position of the Black King. Even though the Black King Pawn is guarded, White takes it anyway by *3 NxP*. (Basically, a *sacrifice* is the offer of material for some other kind of advantage.)

DIAGRAM 174

490. You are not expected to determine White's moves in this game (especially White's third move, which is somewhat risky). Nevertheless, I hope you can understand the moves after they are explained. But even more important than understanding the moves is sensing what a chess game is all about—feeling the give and take of battle.

491. Black is faced with a difficult decision—to take the Knight or not?

492. Black tried very hard to analyze the position, but still couldn't decide what to do. He thought: "If I take the Knight, I may be falling into a trap; but if I don't take the Knight, I have allowed White to capture one of my Pawns."

493. In situations like statement 492—when the best move isn't clear—try to determine the most practical course of action.

494. The most practical course of action is to take the Knight because Black cannot determine why the sacrifice is being offered. That puts the burden on White to prove that the sacrifice is sound.

495. Rely on your own powers. If you can't see the point of a particular move, assume one doesn't exist.

496. If you rely on your own powers, either one of two good things could happen: You could be right, or you could be wrong and your opponent will teach you something! (An old chess maxim says that the best way to prove a sacrifice is wrong is to accept it.)

497. To learn how to play well you should be willing to lose many games. You should be willing to take chances.

498. In our particular game, Black takes the Knight and learns something! He plays *3 . . . PxN*.

DIAGRAM 175

499. Now that the White Knight is off the diagonal of the White Queen, White plays *4 Q–R5ch*.

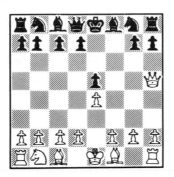

DIAGRAM 176

500. Whether White's sacrifice is sound or not, at least there is a point to it: White is forking both the Black King and the Black King Pawn and also feels that he has powerful attacking chances.

501. In general, don't sacrifice without good reason.

502. In diagram 176 Black can shield his King by 4 . . . P–KN3 (diagram 177), but that would allow White to give a new fork by 5 QxKPch (diagram 178), winning the Black Rook on KR8 after Black gets his King out of check.

DIAGRAM 177   **DIAGRAM 178**

503. So Black didn't play 4 . . . P–KN3 and instead decided to weather the storm and move his King, giving up the right to castle. Black plays *4 . . .* **K–K2.**

DIAGRAM 179

504. White wins a second Pawn for his sacrificed Knight and continues to attack the Black King by *5* **QxKPch.**

DIAGRAM 180

505. Black has only one move to get out of check: *5 . . .* **K–B2.**

DIAGRAM 181

506. The badly exposed Black King should be attacked as much as possible. White has 5 reasonable moves to check the Black King: 4 by the Queen (from Q5, KR5, KB4, and KB5) and 1 by the Bishop (from QB4).

507. Instead of wasting time by attacking with the same piece (the Queen), White should check with the Bishop and bring a new piece into play. White plays *6 B–B4ch.*

DIAGRAM 182

508. When you attack, mobilize as many different pieces as you can. In our present game, it seems foolish to

have the White Queen do what can be done just as well by the White Bishop.

509. Black could block the check to his King by 6 . . . P–Q4 (diagram 183), but that would lose another Pawn after 7 BxPch (diagram 184).

DIAGRAM 183   DIAGRAM 184

510. So Black decides not to play 6 . . . P–Q4 and instead plays the only other legal move he has: *6 . . . **K–N3.***

DIAGRAM 185

511. With the Black King so exposed, it is hard for White to go wrong. White chooses to drive the Black King to the edge of the board by *7* **Q–B5ch.**

DIAGRAM 186

512. Since the White Queen is protected by the Pawn on K4, it can't be captured by the Black King. Therefore, Black has only one legal move: *7* . . . **K–R3.**

DIAGRAM 187

513. Once again, White ignores a couple of reasonable Queen checks (on KB4 and KR3) and instead brings a new piece to bear on the Black King with

8 **P–Q4ch.** White's Queen Bishop is now checking the King.

DIAGRAM 188

514. White's eighth move illustrates a kind of tactic not mentioned before—a discovered attack.

515. A *discovered attack* is a tactic by which one chessman moves out of the way to uncover another chessman's line of attack. The stationary chessman gives the discovered attack. Usually, the moving chessman also gives an attack. Therefore, discovered attacks are often double attacks.

516. The most powerful form of discovered attack—the one that occurs in our game—is a *discovered check*.

517. Black has 2 moves to get out of check: He can block the check with his Queen (Q–N4) or he can block the check with a Pawn (P–KN4). Since Q–N4 allows mate in one move (QxQ mate), Black instead plays *8 . . .* **P–KN4.**

DIAGRAM 189

518. Now if White takes the Pawn on KN5 with his Bishop on QB1, Black could then take the White Bishop with his Queen. Diagrams 190–191 illustrate these moves.

DIAGRAM 190   DIAGRAM 191

519. Since the resulting position is thus unclear, White doesn't play 9 BxPch. He sees that the Pawn on KN5 is pinned to the Black King by the Bishop on QB1. The Pawn is temporarily stuck there.

520. *Question:* What should you try to do to a pinned chessman?

521. *Answer:* Attack it again, especially with a Pawn. Thus, White plays *9* **P–KR4**, at least threatening to fork the Black King and Black Queen by 10 BxPch.

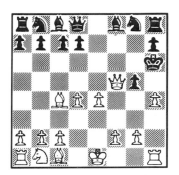

DIAGRAM 192

522. Here Black could have played 9 . . . B–N5ch (diagram 193), but White could easily have protected himself by blocking the check with 10 P–B3 (diagram 194). That forces the Black Bishop to move again, so Black would simply be wasting time.

DIAGRAM 193   DIAGRAM 194

523. Not every check is good. Don't give a check simply because it is a check. (Don't pass bad checks.)

524. Instead of giving the check, Black protects his Pawn by *9 . . .* **B–K2**.

DIAGRAM 195

525. Here White surprises Black. Instead of checking with his dark square Bishop, 10 BxPch, he plays *10* **PxPch**.

DIAGRAM 196

526. This is no ordinary check, for Black is actually being checked twice—by the Pawn on KN5 and by the Rook on KR1. Therefore it is a double check.

527. *Double check* is a special form of discovered attack by which both the moving and stationary attackers give check.

528. Since the only way to get out of double check is to move the King, Black's sole legal response is *10 . . .* **K–N2**.

DIAGRAM 197

529. Look very closely, for White can play and mate Black on this move.

530. The only way to give mate on this move is *11* **Q–B7 mate**.

DIAGRAM 198

531. It is mate because—

(a) the White Queen checks the Black King,
(b) the White Queen cannot be captured by the Black King because it is protected by the White Bishop on QB4,
(c) the White Queen can't be blocked by any Black chessmen,
(d) the Black King cannot escape to a safe square (all potential escape squares are guarded by White),
(e) the Black King is going to be captured on the next move.

532. To get more out of the game, play it over again. But don't try to memorize each move and each comment. Try to understand the spirit of White's attack.

533. In particular, note that White moved five different pieces and three different Pawns. In the final position, Black has only one developed piece (the Bishop).

534. Clearly, White didn't just attack Black—White overwhelmed Black!

535. Black never had time to complete his development because his King was under constant attack.

536. Also, White didn't just check the Black King pointlessly. With 4 of his moves, White was able to check Black and develop new pieces at the same time (the Queen, the two Bishops, and the Rook).

537. After his opening mistakes, Black seemed virtually helpless. From this, perhaps you can see the virtue of aggressive play. It ties up your opponent.

538. Don't worry if some of the ideas in this game escape you. For now, just try to gain a feeling of what chess is.

8	QR8	QN8	QB8	Q8	K8	KB8	KN8	KR8	1
7	QR7	QN7	QB7	Q7	K7	KB7	KN7	KR7	2
6	QR6	QN6	QB6	Q6	K6	KB6	KN6	KR6	3
5	QR5	QN5	QB5	Q5	K5	KB5	KN5	KR5	4
4	QR4	QN4	QB4	Q4	K4	KB4	KN4	KR4	5
3	QR3	QN3	QB3	Q3	K3	KB3	KN3	KR3	6
2	QR2	QN2	QB2	Q2	K2	KB2	KN2	KR2	7
1	QR1	QN1	QB1	Q1	K1	KB1	KN1	KR1	8

White

CHAPTER 8

More Chess Thinking

539. It is convenient to divide a chess game into three separate parts, called *phases*. The three phases are:

(a) The *opening*
(b) The *middle game*
(c) The *endgame*

540. There are no clear boundary lines between the phases. Instead, there are subtle transitions that are often hard to see and understand.

541. Each phase is described differently. The opening is the building phase, the middle game is the planning phase, and the endgame is the exploiting phase. These descriptions are mainly true, but are not absolute.

542. For example: Mistakes can be exploited in the opening and pieces can be developed in the endgame. However, it does seem that each phase has its own character.

543. In the opening you gather the forces and prepare for action.

544. In the middle game you form a sound plan.

545. In the endgame you use your advantages and minimize your weaknesses.

546. What might not be important in one phase may be significant in another.

547. For example: An extra Pawn is seldom important in the opening but almost always important in the endgame.

548. Most endgames are decided by a Pawn reaching the other side to become a new Queen. The side with an extra Queen is almost always able to force mate.

549. Sometimes, both sides try to push their Pawns through to make new Queens. In that case, whoever makes a new Queen first usually wins.

550. A wasted move in the endgame can be critical because it may allow the other side to make a new Queen first.

551. Consequently, the endgame has little to do with mate and much to do with Pawn promotion.

552. In the endgame, mate is rarely seen because most players resign after the other side makes a new Queen. (The chances of winning after this are very slim.)

553. Mate happens far more frequently in the opening and middle game, especially after one side makes a terrible mistake. In the endgame, there usually aren't enough pieces left to exploit serious mistakes in the same way. (Successful mating attacks almost always need at least two pieces and a Queen.)

554. Although endgame study is important, you may find its nature too discouraging. Therefore, I recommend that you skip endgame study until you've had more experience.

555. The opening is the easiest and most practical phase to study because—

   (a) you always start with the same position,
   (b) you don't need much experience to play it reasonably well,
   (c) you get more practice with it (every game must have an opening, but not necessarily a middle game and an endgame—our 11-move game didn't have either a middle game or an endgame),
   (d) you encounter the most important principles at once—centralization and development.

556. The middle game should also be considered early, but it is harder to play and understand than the opening. The middle game stresses planning, logic, and reason—the hallmarks of chess itself.

557. To play the middle game well (or chess for that matter), you must know how to examine a chess position. Examining some middle game positions can be quite difficult.

558. But even in a confused middle game, when you have no idea of what to do, you can still find a reasonable course of action.

559. The solution is to ask questions (in your head, of course). The right set of questions should enable you to begin to form a plan.

560. In chess it is usually better to have a bad plan than none at all.

561. Certain questions can help you to form a plan, regardless of the position.

562. For example, when it is your turn to move, start thinking by asking questions such as these:

(a) Does my opponent's last move threaten me in any way? If so, can I deal with it?

(b) Are any of my chessmen attacked? If so, are they protected enough times? Should I protect them further? Should I trade or move away?

(c) If I have to protect, can I protect with a Pawn? (The best protection is the least valuable chessman available.)

(d) Did I have a threat with my previous move? If so, did my opponent respond to it?

(e) If both of us have a threat, whose is more serious? Whose comes first?

(f) If I have to defend, can I threaten and defend at the same time?

(g) If no one is threatening anything, can I threaten something? Can I improve my position?

(h) Is my King safe? Have I completed my development?

(i) Are my Rooks on open files?

(j) Does my opponent have weaknesses? If so, how can I attack them?

(k) Can I prevent my opponent from castling?

(l) Do I have a plan? If not, can I form a plan? Should I change my plan?

(m) Does my opponent have any annoying checks that I haven't considered? Is there anything important I haven't considered?

563. These questions are just a sample of the kinds that can be asked. It is not necessary to ask them all or in those particular ways. Some of them may not apply to your situation.

564. You are not expected to answer all these questions completely. Just by trying to answer them, you will become more aware of different possibilities and solutions.

565. The process of asking questions to determine a course of action is known as the *analytic method*.

566. Although the analytic method is particularly valuable in middle games, it is helpful throughout the entire game.

567. Even if at first you find it hard to answer your own questions, ask them anyway. With experience you will be able to answer them. Asking questions is the fastest way to learn about chess reasoning and thus to improve.

568. You can't exploit what you can't express. Make sure you translate all chess ideas into words. (One Soviet

chess teacher goes so far as to say that if a plan can't be expressed in words, it doesn't even exist.)

LOOK AT WHAT YOU'RE DOING!

569.	You may think that good players should beat you in just a few moves, but you'll find that most of the time they will need about 20 moves to do it. To win quickly you must take chances. Since experienced players aren't willing to risk losing to a novice, most short games are won by bad players rather than good ones.

570.	This section presents three games in which the winners take chances and get away with them. The games are given with comments to show both the careless mistakes and what should have been done instead.

571.	Upon finishing this book, you may want to continue learning about chess. To give you practice following recorded moves, the three games and their notes are presented without diagrams, as they might appear in advanced works. You will have to play out the moves on your own board!

572.	The moves of each game are introduced in score sheet fashion and are followed by numbered explanatory comments. For each game, I recommend that you play the moves and read the comments starting from the White side first, alternating with the moves and comments from the Black side (merely turn the board around).

573. Pretend that you are playing against real opponents. Some people even try to guess the moves by holding an index card over them before looking. By trying to guess the moves for both White and Black, you see more clearly that chess is a game of interaction.

GAME 1

WHITE		BLACK
1	**P–K4**	**P–K4**
2	**B–B4**	**N–QB3**
3	**Q–B3**	**N–Q5**
4	**QxP mate**	

574. *1* **P–K4:** A good developing move for it opens the way for the Queen and King Bishop and also strikes at the center.

575. *1 . . .* **P–K4:** Good for the same reasons as White's move.

576. *2* **B–B4:** Though this move develops the Bishop toward the center, you should develop the Kingside Knight before the Kingside Bishop. Besides, on 2 N–KB3 White would be attacking the Black King Pawn.

577. *2 . . .* **N–QB3:** A reasonable developing move, but better would be 2 . . . N–KB3, attacking the White King Pawn.

578. *3 Q–B3?*: A bad move, for unless there is a good reason, don't bring out the Queen early. White plays this move because it threatens mate at KB7, but doesn't realize that Black can easily deal with the threat and build his position at the same time by 3 . . . N–B3. This alternate move would get a new piece out, strike at the center, and block the attack of the White Queen.

579. *3 . . . N–Q5?*: This is a mistake that allows mate in one move. Instead of responding to the White threat at Black's KB2, Black goes ahead with his own plans by attacking the White Queen. Don't ignore your opponent's threats.

580. *4 QxP mate:* There is no way for Black to avoid capture of his King on the next move. While White won quickly, he really didn't earn the victory. White won on his opponent's oversight, not on his own ability. The lesson: Don't ignore your opponent's moves.

GAME 2

	WHITE	BLACK
1	P–K4	P–K4
2	N–KB3	N–KB3
3	NxP	NxP
4	Q–K2	N–KB3
5	N–B6ch	B–K2
6	NxQ	resigns

581.   *1* **P–K4:** See game 1 (statement 574).

582.   *1 . . .* **P–K4:** See game 1 (statement 575).

583.   *2* **N–KB3:** The best move here, for it develops the Knight toward the center and attacks the Black King Pawn. It also prepares for castling Kingside by getting the Knight off the back rank.

584.   *2 . . .* **N–KB3:** Good for the same reasons as White's second move, but it doesn't protect the attacked King Pawn. While this move is adequate for experienced players, you should play 2 . . . N–QB3 instead, defending the Pawn. In this case, Black is merely trying to copy White's play, and that's a bad idea. After all, if White mates first, the game is over.

585.   *3* **NxP:** Capturing a valuable center Pawn. Whenever you can win material without too much trouble, you should.

586.   *3 . . .* **NxP:** Copying White, move for move. Experienced players know that in this position Black has to play 3 . . . P–Q3, driving the White Knight back first. Then Black can recapture his Pawn. Obviously, beginners can't know all the complexities of copycat play. Don't copy, unless you really know what you're doing.

587.   *4* **Q–K2:** Now Black sees that if he responds with 4 . . . Q–K2 himself, White takes the Black Knight first and protects his own Knight in the process.

588. *4 . . . N–KB3?:* This move loses the Queen. Any other move would also put Black in a poor position. Study the actual position closely (after this move) and you'll see that the White Queen and the Black King are on the same file, screened from each other by the White Knight on K5. If White moves the Knight away, his Queen discovers check to the Black King. But where should White move the Knight to?

589. *5 N–B6ch!:* The Knight attacks the Black Queen and is safe from capture because Black is also in check from the White Queen. Black can't save his Queen because he must get out of check.

590. *5 . . . B–K2:* The Queen could not be saved by 5 . . . Q–K2, for the White Knight could still take it.

591. *6 NxQ:* Black resigns because he really doesn't have enough compensation for his Queen. The lesson: Don't blindly copy your opponent's moves.

GAME 3

WHITE		BLACK
1	P–K4	P–K4
2	N–KB3	N–QB3
3	B–B4	N–Q5
4	NxP	Q–N4
5	NxKBP	QxNP
6	R–B1	QxKPch
7	B–K2	N–B6 mate

592. *1* **P–K4:** See game 1 (statement 574).

593. *1 . . .* **P–K4:** See game 1 (statement 575).

594. *2* **N–KB3:** See game 2 (statement 583).

595. *2 . . .* **N–QB3:** This is the best way to defend the King Pawn for it develops a piece toward the center. Another good way to protect the King Pawn, not played in this game, is 2 . . . P–Q3.

596. *3* **B–B4:** This develops the Bishop to a square within the enlarged center. From QB4 the Bishop attacks the weakest point in the uncastled Black position, the KB2 square. This is the weakest square because it is defended only by the King, the most vulnerable piece.

597. *3 . . .* **N–Q5?:** This move is questionable for several reasons. Since it doesn't really threaten any White chessmen (the two it attacks are adequately defended), N–Q5 wastes time. In the opening you should try to bring out as many different pieces as soon as you can. You can't bring out all your pieces if you keep moving the same one. Actually, Black is hoping that White will play a move that looks good but really isn't (4 NxP). Instead, White should play either 4 NxN, removing the prematurely advanced Knight, or 4 P–B3, forcing it to move again.

598. *4* **NxP?:** White is biting at the bait. It is easy to become blinded by the sight of an undefended Pawn.

Taking a Pawn without looking at the consequences is called *Pawn grabbing*, a mistake that chess players of all levels are likely to make.

599. *4 . . . Q–N4:* This is a double attack. Both the Knight on K5 and the Pawn on KN2 are threatened by the Black Queen. Which chessman is White going to save?

600. *5 NxKBP:* White saves the Knight and also gives his own double attack. The Knight now forks the Queen on KN4 and the Rook on KR1. But Black has seen further ahead than White and punishes him badly for his Pawn grabbing.

601. *5 . . . QxNP:* Black threatens to take the Rook on KR1 with check. Although White is losing anyway (because his King is too endangered), he can prolong the struggle by defending his KP with 6 P–Q3. However, Black would have to make large mistakes for White to get even.

602. *6 R–B1?:* White saves the Rook but is losing quickly. As in the previous statement, White can desperately try to hold on with 6 P–Q3 instead.

603. *6 . . . QxKPch:* Now White has only two ways to get out of check. He can block the check by 7 Q–K2 (losing the Queen to 7 . . . NxQ) or he can play 7 B–K2 as in the actual game.

604.   *7 B–K2:* Since losing the Queen is equivalent to resigning, White plays this move, hoping that Black doesn't see the best response.

605.   *7 . . .* **N–B6 mate!:** Notice that the Knight can't be captured by the Bishop for the Bishop is pinned to the King by the Black Queen. This kind of Knight mate is called a *smothered mate* because the losing King is smothered by his own chessmen. The lesson: Don't grab Pawns without considering the consequences.

	Black

8	QR1 QR8	QN1 QN8	QB1 QB8	Q1 Q8	K1 K8	KB1 KB8	KN1 KN8	KR1 KR8	1
7	QR2 QR7	QN2 QN7	QB2 QB7	Q2 Q7	K2 K7	KB2 KB7	KN2 KN7	KR2 KR7	2
6	QR3 QR6	QN3 QN6	QB3 QB6	Q3 Q6	K3 K6	KB3 KB6	KN3 KN6	KR3 KR6	3
5	QR4 QR5	QN4 QN5	QB4 QB5	Q4 Q5	K4 K5	KB4 KB5	KN4 KN5	KR4 KR5	4
4	QR5 QR4	QN5 QN4	QB5 QB4	Q5 Q4	K5 K4	KB5 KB4	KN5 KN4	KR5 KR4	5
3	QR6 QR3	QN6 QN3	QB6 QB3	Q6 Q3	K6 K3	KB6 KB3	KN6 KN3	KR6 KR3	6
2	QR7 QR2	QN7 QN2	QB7 QB2	Q7 Q2	K7 K2	KB7 KB2	KN7 KN2	KR7 KR2	7
1	QR8 QR1	QN8 QN1	QB8 QB1	Q8 Q1	K8 K1	KB8 KB1	KN8 KN1	KR8 KR1	8

White

CONCLUSION

606. You've probably understood some points and not understood others in the course of learning how to play chess. This is natural in the study of any subject.

607. Yet certain principles and practical suggestions should be reread, reconsidered, and remembered:

    (a) Be aggressive

    (b) Don't ignore enemy moves

(c) Move with reason
(d) Centralize
(e) In the opening, move only the central Pawns
(f) Attack in number
(g) Mobilize all the pieces
(h) Develop with threats
(i) Knights before Bishops
(j) Castle early
(k) Don't bring the Queen out early
(l) Control the open lines
(m) Try to win material
(n) Don't sacrifice without reason
(o) Look for double attacks
(p) Make practical decisions
(q) Don't give pointless checks
(r) Think ahead
(s) Don't waste moves
(t) Rely on your own powers
(u) Plan, but don't be afraid to change your plan
(v) Think in words
(w) Don't play bad moves on purpose
(x) Don't rush your moves (take your time and think)
(y) Ask questions

608. Memorize this list if you memorize anything. But don't think that chess is just an intellectual exercise. It is a great game.

609. If you studied football, but never played, do you think you'd be a good football player?

610. Play chess with friends and make new friends who play chess. Try to teach the game to others. This will strengthen your own grasp of the game. Join a chess club if your neighborhood has one. Either your local library or the nearest school should be able to tell you if a club exists. (Both may have chess clubs.)

611. Read other chess books. You may have a problem choosing the right one, because more books have been written about chess than all other games combined! However, many of the problems you will encounter can be answered by referring back to *Let's Play Chess!*

612. Join the United States Chess Federation. That will enable you to play in rated tournaments and to receive *Chess Life,* the official monthly magazine of chess in America. Write:
    United States Chess Federation
    186 Route 9W
    New Windsor, NY 12550

613. Play postal chess. Games can be arranged by the U.S. Chess Federation or by yourself privately. It can be a lot of fun waiting for the weekly moves to come in from around the world, across the country, or down the block.

614. If you have more specific questions about chess, send them with a stamped, self-addressed envelope to:
    The Chess Institute
    23 West 10th Street
    New York, NY 10011

615. One final word: When actually playing chess, pretend I'm looking over your shoulder. Before making a move, try to explain its point to me (in your head, of course). Trying to explain your moves will force you to think more concretely.

616. It's time to move out the first Pawn. *Let's Play Chess!*

Index

About the Author

BRUCE PANDOLFINI is a U.S. National Chess Master and Executive Director of the Chess Institute at the Marshall Chess Club in New York City. He is also a member of the faculty of the New School for Social Research in New York. He has delivered more than 1,000 lectures on chess and has given more than 7,000 private lessons, many of them to children. Bruce analyzed the match for the world championship between Bobby Fischer and Boris Spassky on National Educational Television and is a columnist for *Chess Life*.